THE JUMP

*From Chaos To Clarity For
Your Striving Small Business*

By Jason Scott Montoya

© 2019 by Jason Scott Montoya

Published by Protheseos Inc.

ISBN-13: 978-1095023235
ISBN-10: 1095023233
First Printing: 2019

No part of this publication may be reproduced, stored in a retrieval system, or transmitted in any form or by any means—for example, electronic, photocopy, recording—without the prior written permission of the publisher. The only exception is brief quotations in printed reviews.

Scripture quotations are taken from the Holy Bible, New Living Translation, copyright ©1996, 2004, 2007, 2013, 2015 by Tyndale House Foundation. Used by permission of Tyndale House Publishers, Inc., Carol Stream, Illinois 60188. All rights reserved.

For additional resources, please visit www.jasonscottmontoya.com/jump

Contents

An Introduction By My Friend, A Small Business Owner

7

Part 1: Understanding The Situation

Chapter 1: Facing The Chasm

15

Chapter 2: A Powerful Plan To Move The Entrepreneur's Stalling Small Business Forward

17

Chapter 3: The Five Natural Stages Of Every Organization

41

Chapter 4: The Jump - From Rogue Action Management (*Chaos*) To System Oriented Leadership (*Order*)

53

Chapter 5: The Noodlehead Marketing Story

101

Part 2: Moving Forward

Chapter 6: Step One - Transform Your Business By Leveling Yourself Up

113

Chapter 7: Step Two - Build A Strong Business Foundation

187

Chapter 8: Step Three - Lead Your Dedicated Team Forward

249

Chapter 9: Step Four - Elevate Your Business With Bullet-Proof Systems & Mental Models

289

Chapter 10: A Five-Phase Process For Transforming Your Messy Business Into A Well-Oiled Machine

331

Chapter 11: My Parting Words To The Visionary Business Owner

363

Chapter 12: Standing On The Edge

373

Epilogue By My Small Business Owning Friend

375

*Dedicated To My Loving, Loyal,
And Lasting Wife, Cait.*

An Introduction By My Friend, A Small Business Owner

It was a typical day at the office. I was drinking coffee, socializing with my staff, attending meetings, and doing the do-ables. Even if things weren't perfect, I felt like everything in the business was holding together.

But it wouldn't last.

Our annual meeting with the bank didn't go well, and they moved us to their *"Special Assets"* program (*also known as "The hospital group"*). This meant that there was a chance they would not renew our million dollar line of credit.

We lived on that line of credit.

Uh oh.

The truth is, we were unhealthy, and the bank was right to be concerned.

For me, the business had slowly gotten harder. The fun was gone.

"Things will get better," I'd tell myself.

"If we keep working hard, we'll catch a break." But, the wheels were slowly falling off, and like the frog slowly cooking in a pot of heating water, I wasn't aware of what was happening around me.

The bank's action was the swift kick in the pants I needed, but it didn't stop me from going home depressed and a little panicked (*ok, a lot panicked*).

Since the inception of our business, we grew an average of one million dollars per year for thirteen years and then plateaued for five straight years.

What started off feeling like being on a rocket ship turned into feeling like being stranded on the moon.

For five years straight, we tried everything to get unstuck. We threw resources (*time and money*) at all the things that worked before, but everything we did failed to gain traction.

It was like the person who tries to get out of a hole by continuing to dig, and by doing so, worsened the problems. Chaos grew with less direction, sporadic activity, lack of direction, fewer leaders, less profit, and higher expenses.

From 2014 to 2019, my bursts of energy and intense effort consistently pushed me to severe burnout. In these moments of exhaustion, I spent my drive time, shower time, and bed time thinking about how I could get out of this mess — by just selling the whole thing.

"I am just not made for this," I'd tell myself. *"I don't want to do this anymore. I don't enjoy it. I'd rather live under a bridge without this stress. I'll go to work for someone. I'll be a consultant. I'll do — anything but this."*

I began to imagine what I would do if I successfully sold the business.

What would I do with the money?

I wouldn't stick it in the stock market; I am an entrepreneur and need to be **DOING** something. Perhaps, I could invest in other businesses. No, I wouldn't blindly trust someone else like that.

"What if I bought an entire business?" Yes! That makes sense. I'd want to buy a business in the right industry, but the owner doesn't know how to scale or is burned out. It'd be a *"turnaround"* situation; not very profitable now, but with a great deal of potential.

Wait!

"That's what I already have!"

Around and around, I'd go like this — for years. I enjoyed the actual work; I just hated *"running the business."*

I left the bank meeting deflated and depressed. Numb, I wasn't sure what I was going to do, and for perhaps the first time I wasn't sure I cared. I'd reached the bottom.

This feeling, this moment of rock bottom — feeling stuck and helpless, or defeated, may be where you are right now.

Let me ask you some questions.

- Are you tempted to sell, close, or quit your business?
- Do you know why you started down this road?
- Do you know what you want from your business?
- Are you wondering how it could get you there?

While the rewards of business ownership are numerous, there are challenges and obstacles we face due to poor decisions, neglect, and external circumstances that we can't always control. On this roller coaster journey, we may feel invincible one minute and doubtful and depressed the next. As we struggle to get unstuck and move forward, we often feel overwhelmed and unequipped. When we overcome our denial, we'll look in the mirror and see the things we've not been ready or willing to change.

It would have been a tremendous help if someone shared with me what to expect along the way, how to navigate these entrepreneurial challenges, and what it **REALLY** takes to make it work.

And that's where this book, and its author come into your story.

Jason and I met in 2005 when he and his wife moved to Atlanta. We, along with our wives, hit it off right away. We played and worked together over the years, including through my business, CablesAndKits. He worked as a temp employee in the warehouse, as a marketing contractor helping to grow our online platform, and now as a trusted and valued consultant helping to build and shape our leaders, relationships, and culture. We've both grown significantly since when we first met years ago.

For many years I watched and cheered as Jason figured out life, marriage, business, and his walk with the Lord. I watched his life get torn apart through neglect and poor decision making, and then rebuilt from the inside-out, better and stronger.

It was hard to watch at times, yet also inspiring (*and encouraging*). He's certainly the type of open leader who leans into living as a public example for a better outcome and to model life for others.

And this journey, Jason's example, and the lessons learned are how he shares his transition from a chaotic world to one of order, structure, and discipline. He's built a life of predictable results in his personal economy, and for his clients.

His transformation is nothing short of spectacular, and he is truly a model and inspiration to me and those that know him.

If he can make the Jump, so can you.

Enjoy the book.

Craig Haynie

Note: Craig continues sharing his insights and wisdom, stuff you'll explore throughout the book, in his own words, and for your continued benefit, in the book's epilogue.

> *Craig is the founder and CEO of **CablesAndKits.com**, a distributor and retailer of network hardware and cabling infrastructure. Connect with Craig at linkedin.com/in/craighaynie.*

Part One: Understanding The Situation

1. Facing The Chasm
2. A Powerful Plan To Move The Entrepreneur's Stalling Small Business Forward
3. The Five Natural Stages Of Every Organization
4. The Jump: From Rogue Action Management (*Chaos*) To System Oriented Leadership (*Order*)
5. The Noodlehead Marketing Story

1. Facing The Chasm

As I stood on the edge of the gorge, I looked out across the horizon, wondering if I could make my small business successful.

Do I turn back now, or make the jump?

Before, it was an easy question to answer. Now, I wasn't sure.

Years earlier, nothing could stop my wife and I as we boldly moved from Arizona to Atlanta, zealously pursuing our entrepreneurial dreams.

With an abundance of potential ahead, we leaned in hard and fast in a variety of directions to make our mark, launch the company, and sustain a business that would facilitate our personal and professional aspirations.

Slowly and surely, the tension and friction of entrepreneurship began to take its toll on me, our marriage, and company. The momentum and energy moving in our favor were rapidly shifting directions as it slowly began crushing us with it's increasing weight.

The challenges escalated, and the doubt crept in. Was I capable of making the dream happen? Was it impossible for me to build a business foundation that would attract and empower a great team? Was having a sustainable ecosystem simply a pipedream?

I was stuck, standing on the edge.

On the other side of the chasm before me were my hopes, dreams, and aspirations. Out of reach, the other side felt like an impossible distance away.

As I considered going back the way I came, I Imagined a failed entrepreneur who gave up when it was too hard. Was I a problem solver who couldn't figure out a solution?

I felt trapped.

Should I walk back to 'safety' or **should I jump?**

2. A Powerful Plan To Move The Entrepreneur's Stalling Small Business Forward

Bang! That was me hitting the invisible ceiling with Noodlehead Marketing, my established small marketing company. We had grown year-over-year until finally, I hit my limit.

My approach to leading and managing got me to my current level of success, and it kept me busy, but it wasn't moving us forward, towards sustainability and growth. **For three years straight, our company income was stagnant, and we couldn't get over the hump.**

It turns out; this stuck point is a common occurrence with founders. How we initially fueled our success worked, but this same way fails to sustain and grow. *Something is missing.*

Rather than being content with the success we have, we are frustrated we can't elevate beyond this ceiling. Instead of dealing with the root issues, we become easily distracted, chasing shiny objects (*ideas, opportunities, people, and technology*) to alleviate symptoms but fail to reach that elusive sustainability.

Thus, founders enter into years of wandering in circles. They're changing things, shuffling people and systems around, but are never genuinely moving the business forward. This unfolding change can last years, *and for a handful of founders who fail to address the root problems, decades.*

The problems are not exclusive to the business owner. The leadership, team, and vendors also lack clarity, and without it, quickly check out or take advantage of the situation. If power players continue to benefit from this aimless wandering in some personal way, why should anyone bother changing it?

Like finding ourselves on the map at the mall, our first step in the process of moving out of this stagnation is to understand the stages of an organization and where you and your company currently reside on that map. We can then discover how we go from where we are to where we want to be.

This book is my way to go back in time and share the key insights I needed to hear while running my small business, but with you instead of my past self as the recipient (*since I don't have access to a time machine*). It's the blueprint I wished for but didn't have.

The Five Natural Stages of Every Organization

While it feels chaotic when we traverse through the journey of business ownership, there is a pattern that illuminates the stages of an organization.

The first stage begins with a lightbulb moment. Every new business starts as an idea — an exciting moment of revelation.

> *"This could be a business!"*

With promise, we play with and talk about the idea internally and with others. With enough potential, we seriously explore what it takes to make the idea real. If the variables stack up well or we gain traction, we launch the business.

With business growth comes a season of pushing it forward, as we strive to sustain it. We hit bumps along the way, and during those choppy seasons, we re-evaluate how we're doing things and focus on improving. Moreover, if we're to continue, we focus on making the business better, shedding what's not working, and adopting what helps us grow.

This summary illustrates the IDEMA [1] framework, a concept we'll tease out throughout the book, and also the framing for the five natural stages.

---

[1] Montoya, Jason: "IDEMA — A Framework For Capturing & Sustaining Ideas." medium.com/@IDEMA

Ideate. **D**iscover. **E**xecute. **M**aintain. **A**udit.

I.D.E.M.A.

By knowing these five important-to-understand stages of an organization, our goal now is to transform this five-stage linear process into a cyclical one.

Within reasonable cycles, we should consistently refine and revise as we move through them. The audit stage is critical to evaluating and acting. With paired action, audits prevent us from fossilizing (*dying while stuck in legacy systems*) as a company.

By keeping the company perpetually moving through all five stages, we ruthlessly focus on what matters and eliminate what doesn't. Different business owners prefer certain stages to others, and they comfortably camp out.

Some love ideas. They come up with new ones like they're going out of style, and many are viable and profitable concepts. However, if they never actually discover (*and eventually execute*) that idea, what good is it?

Others land on a solid idea and **plan it to death.** They map out every step of the process with a contingency plan for every possible scenario. Their pitfall is relishing in their privately written words and never executing on what they've planned.

Executors love to create new things, but never intend or plan to sustain them, so they quickly create wreckage of unfinished and abandoned projects. They never make a long-lasting impact because, by the time they're close to doing so, they're onto the next thing.

Some entrepreneurs **enter and stay in the maintenance stage.** And the moment they do (*without an audit cycle*), they begin the process of becoming bloated (*adding without ever removing*). However, that doesn't come without some form of enabling. Whatever (*client, staff member, money, etc.*) is allowing them to stay in this mode eventually vanishes and when it does, they're not prepared to adapt to the pulled out rug.

Lastly, we have those who **hang out in the audit phase.** These entrepreneurs are continually evaluating, but by staying in this stage, they fuel cynicism and become constant criticizers who don't ever act on their, often useful, insight.

Somewhere in these stages, is where you've camped out. And now, you may be wondering how you navigate these challenges and move forward when you're stuck. *How do you move from chaos to order and from comfort to proactivity?*

You JUMP.

Making The Jump From Rogue Action Management (RAM) To Sustainable System Oriented Leadership (SOL)

It's best to begin a business with proper planning and clear intentions. Unfortunately, startups don't usually begin this way, so founders find themselves several years into the company's journey before they ask foundational questions about their business and the role it plays in their lives.

Years ago, there was a prospective client enamored by the idea of innovating through entrepreneurship and was interested in working with Noodlehead Marketing. We communicated how important it was to establish his intentions and understand why he was pursuing this venture. He proceeded to tell us how he wasn't interested in knowing why he was building the wall, his metaphor for the business; he just wanted to build it. He'd figure out the why later.

Huh? As an outsider, this seemed absurd.

What if the way you're operating your business is not the way you'd do so if you rebooted? What if this is not the business you'd create if you could launch any company? Answering these questions is critical to know your path for making the jump. If making the jump requires everything you have, then you better choose to direct your entire focus on what you care about most.

You better understand *the why*.

It turns out; I was no different from the wall guy. He was just more honest.

When I launched my marketing business, I didn't deliberately discover **why I was beginning** the company, **how we would conduct our work**, and **where it was taking us collectively and individually**. Years later, when I eventually did, it illuminated my shaky foundation upon which I was operating.

> **Key Questions**
> - Why did you originally start your business?
> - Within what guidelines will you operate?
> - What's the endgame for you, your team, and your company?

By not answering these vital questions ahead of time (*because we don't have the answers*), we end up weaving a web of complex alliances, motivations, and goals; think of tangled Christmas lights as an example of how our business operates. The default state of many founders is leaning towards messy chaos, driven by reactive and conflicting endeavors.

Eventually, this friction created by the wild west of entanglement causes the business engine to seize up, and we get stuck in one of the five stages described earlier. We then enter into a perpetual state of planning and not acting, striving and burning out, doing because it's always been done that way, or complaining without making things better.

To not only survive but to thrive we must make the jump from chaos to order, from launching to sustaining, and intentionally moving towards success, instead of allowing the natural current to drive us back towards failure.

The JUMP moves us forward. It's pushing the IDEMA flywheel to ensure we're improving, not decaying. It's our conscious choice to move forward through the cycle even when we want to camp out. It's the actions we take to move out of chaos into a sustainable orderly one. It's the accountability we foster to ensure we don't stagnate.

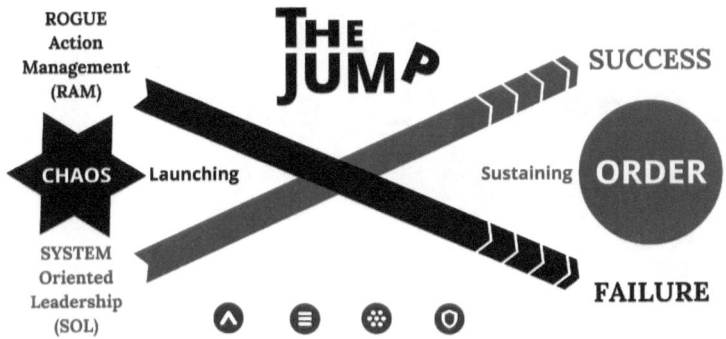

The JUMP requires we lead and manage through effective processes, and minimize the amount of rogue action management (RAM) (*non-system oriented activity*) often required in a startup mode. Think firefighting instead of fireproofing, and busy work instead of productive action.

A profound reality check can do the trick, but for the requirements needed to make the transition successfully, it'll require you, the founder, to evolve as a person and leader.

You won't change your company until you change you.

The change can't just be superficial.

It must go internal.

Step 1: Transform Your Business By Leveling Yourself Up

Several years after launching Noodlehead Marketing, I found myself in a moment of reflection. If I were to start a new marketing business, knowing what I know now, how would it operate? What type of marketing firm would I create?

By this time, the external forces of clients, team members, family, and people with influence over me were profoundly defining the company. The pressure of external forces overrode my intentions.

It was finally time to decide what type of company I was going to create for myself.

This tension came on the tail of a year of a personal identity crisis. My life, my marriage, my faith, and my business were in a stew of chaos. My way of accommodating everyone (*and not getting clear on my intentions*) wasn't working, and the trajectory of my decisions and actions were taking me down a broken and beaten road I had no interest in finishing.

Let me pause for a moment here.

As you're reading the preceding and subsequent sections (*as well as the remainder of the book*), you'll likely wonder why I'm diving into my personal stuff when this book is about company growth and helping business owners.

You might be thinking, *"Can't you just move along to the practical stuff needed to succeed?"*.

The short answer is no. Helping you make the jump is a complicated endeavor. To address the issues, while equipping you to transition from where you are to what you need to become, is no easy matter. It's even more challenging to accomplish this with only written words in a book.

What I do know after working with countless small business owners, and being one myself, is how inevitable problems in a company stem back to the personal stuff from the founder. **To decide and act on what's most important in your business is a subsequent step to doing the same for your life, meaningful relationships, and community.**

When I realized how this personal element was affecting everything around me, including the business, I knew I needed help.

In a desperate prayer, I asked God to show me His way since my inconsistent and accommodating approach was contributing to the problems. After that humble prayer, there was an exodus of unhealthy relationships with new healthy guidance entering my life. Through this transition, I asked and answered personal questions about **who I was**, **my purpose**, **my life's destination** (*vision*), and **how I was to get there** (*mission*).

Key Questions

- On what foundation is your identity-based?
- What is your life's purpose?
- Where do you want to end up?
- How will you get to this place?

It was a monumental moment in my life that required embracing foundational beliefs that would shape my future. While it seems like this exercise would have made my life better, it quickly got worse, at first. Taking a stand and changing means dislodging people around us, which surfaces and amplifies resistance.

These challenges to my firm foundations were unpleasant, but they were the test required to ensure these pillars would stand strong through future severe storms.

With a strong personal foundation, I was now able to go back into the business and face the question in front of me.

What type of business would I intentionally create?

Step 2: Set Up (*or Re-Setup*) Your Business For Success

Behind the most reliable companies are leaders with a clear understanding and security in their personal identity and intentions.

Powerful companies require strong convictions from the founder. Anything less will fade away when it gets hard.

Clearly articulating vision and mission for the company also foster clarity and accountability, two vital ingredients for your business to operate at the highest level. With an articulated vision, followers know where they're going, and they quickly ideate on how to get there effectively. With a mission built on this clarity, you and the staff now have a map to not only point the way but to easily see when the company and its team are operating within the mission and towards the vision. Often the accountability is self-driven by each person.

However, this clarity in the business stems from the same focus in the trajectory of our personal lives. The same exploration we went through with my business followed a season of personal discovery and deeply anchored convictions for the type of leader I wanted to be, and how the company I would lead would help me get there.

This reflection point led to my company's half-time. Looking forward, I had to choose what type of business we were creating, while also asking the right questions to foster clarity.

Key Questions

Why were we in business?

If we were successful, what would the company look like? Within what guidelines would we follow to get there (*did our ends justify any means*)?

How would we get from where we were to where we wanted to be?

We needed four essential ingredients.

Purpose, Vision, Values, and Mission.

Along the way, these concepts were hard for me to grasp, and I struggled to harmonize them with their confusing overlaps. Out of this desire to understand was born a new visualization for communicating purpose, vision, mission, and core values in a unifying way.

The Formula for Intentionality.

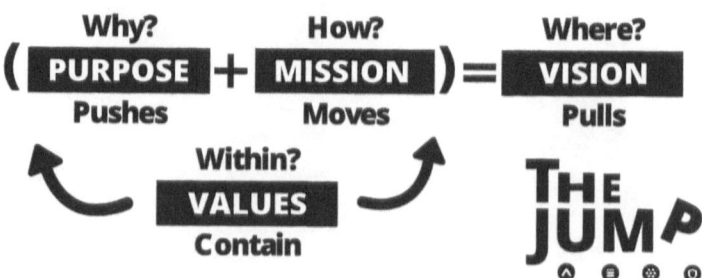

Purpose (*Why?*) plus mission (*How?*) within (*?*) core values equal the creation of our vision (*Where?*).

Both the key questions and the way the formula illuminated the intertwined relationships empowered me to discover these ingredients for myself, my business, and others.

After I explored and anchored my personal answers to these challenging questions, applying these concepts for the company soon followed.

We wrestled, tested, and explored these elements until we arrived at our finalized and written statements.

Through the process, we also dealt with our issues, weaknesses, and pride. Once we did, we quickly made progress in moving towards the vision.

This contrast reminds me of the nation of Israel. When the Israelites left Egypt and traveled to the Promised Land, they wandered for decades. Interestingly, the trip should only have taken thirteen weeks. Likewise, in business, we'll wander for months, years, or decades when getting to where we want to go should only take a small window of time with a clear focus and dependable follow-through.

Eventually, we established these intentions with Noodlehead Marketing. As I share them in a seemingly clear and concise way below, the process to get there was lengthy and challenging.

The purpose of Noodlehead Marketing was *to be an example of excellence and accountability*. Our mission was *to obliterate marketing neglect*. We moved on these intentions within the core values of *passion, love, respect, service, change* (*for the better*), and *openness* (*to share/receive ideas*). Acting this out resulted in our vision of *intentional organizations reflecting excellence* (*how we defined marketing*).

On this foundation, we built a framework of five business units: Planning, Project Facilitation, Communication, Community, & Resources. We clearly defined the intentions (*Why, how, within, & where?*) for both the company and each of these areas (*departments*). We also assigned responsibility to these areas for effective leadership based on our respective strengths.

These directives permeated our organization and leadership was responsible for discovering intentions on their nested departments and projects while also being accountable for making and sustaining these intentions.

With a foundation, we built a framework. With a framework, we assigned responsibility. With clear accountability, we transformed our business from reactive to proactive.

With change comes a tension and difficulty (*even when it's invited*). So, how would our team handle this new structure and direction?

Step 3: Making The Jump With Your Existing Team

When you achieve this newfound clarity, it feels earth-shattering in its impact, but there will be team members that don't understand the value you see in it. There will be others who feel uncomfortable with this clarity and attempt to thwart it, either actively or passively (*for both good and selfish reasons*). The challenge here is navigating the change and bringing the team along.

As a business, we spent years recruiting a team that could survive the chaos of our business. However, we failed at retaining the type of people we needed to create, implement, and maintain the structure.

Our years-long search for an effective project manager eluded us. Those of us who managed to survive within the chaos were unable to change it. The type of person we needed to help us drive projects forward wouldn't last in our rogue action management (*RAM*) culture.

A few months after landing a seasoned project manager, I went on vacation to Disney World. In the middle of my trip, I received a phone call from a team member that this project manager couldn't handle the chaos anymore and left, without explanation.

It reminded me of another project manager friend I had brought on in the early years of the business. One weekend we were in the middle of a highly demanding project, and things were not going well. That weekend, he up and left, and to this day, I've never heard from him.

Those of us that remained were good at working in chaos. It was not a healthy way to work, and we were not yet equipped to change it.

The type of person we needed couldn't healthily exist in our crazy context. When I finally embraced this reality, I sat us all down and directed us to figure out how we must work together to foster the environment needed to prevent these types of people from running away screaming and instead pursue working with us.

Subsequently, we quickly explored the journey every project goes through, and we mapped it out. The result was IDEMA, the framework discussed earlier for capturing and sustaining ideas.

With this roadmap in place, we looked at each other and decided, based on our strengths, what roles we all could each play when it came to managing our projects as well as our client's activities.

Instead of finding the perfect person who could do it all, we found the ideal roles we could each play in the larger picture. We did it together.

Imagine a relay race where a team member carried the baton towards another. They'd overlap while running as they handed off the rod. This team-oriented approach was the method we shifted for leading and managing our projects. We went from *needing* a project manager to no longer seeking one. We became a *project management team*.

While there was a frustrating transition (*and some people didn't come along*), it fostered a planning and execution squad that would build sustainable systems. The satisfaction of us doing it together, and without finding that unicorn project manager, was powerful.

Step 4: Creating Long-Lasting Visible Systems To Bulletproof Your Business

If you're not around to lead your business, how well does it continue to operate? When the founder's (*or specific team member's*) activity is tightly intertwined with their success or failure, it's easy and quick for them to burn out.

During the extended process of shutting down my marketing business (*more on that in chapter 5*), I performed technology and file spring cleaning. From when I began the company to the day it ended, I was continually building systems to manage projects and move things forward. What I quickly recognized was how often I would create the same system over and over again in different ways.

I never had the discipline and memory to stick with the good things we built. Instead, we created and forgot about them. When we realized we needed them *again*, we made them *again*. We struggled to gain traction because we did the same basic things repeatedly (*what a waste!*).

There was a shift when I created a blueprint for the business and input every single internal project we had going on in it. After listing hundreds of items, it was quickly apparent how overcommitted we were. **We were trying to do everything, and as a result, we had wreckage of unfinished, decaying, and abandoned projects.**

The power of creating a blueprint for company-wide visibility not only acted as a much-needed reality check for this visionary (*me*), it also created a connected dashboard for us to know the direction of the company, how it was segmented, roles and responsibilities, and the progress of nested projects (*Those many little projects make or break a business*).

With the destination in place, an informed and directed team, and the founding of a long-lasting system, the next step in the process was transitioning the organization into something great.

How do we move from the current chaos into an orderly and effective business model? How do we go beyond the perpetual startup cycle and create a sustainable company?

Make the JUMP: A Five-Phase Process For Transforming Your Messy Business Into a Well-Oiled Machine

Successfully making the jump requires a soup of vital ingredients. We must understand the business cycle and our propensity to get stuck in the wheel's cogs. From this revelation, we'll embrace becoming the leader our revitalized company requires. Plus, we'll commit to the long-lasting systems, and bring our existing team members (*at least those that choose to continue*) along.

We'll also do the heavy lifting of knowing who we want to become, and create a framework to move towards it. It's with this stage set that we can not only make the jump but successfully stay where we land. Moreover, do it over and over, as necessary to adapt to changing circumstances.

With the ingredients in place, we'll embrace the following five phases and move the company forward in a way that progresses long-term benefits while addressing short-term requirements. We need to fuel the transition from the very beginning.

Here's how it goes.

1. **Tackle Low Hanging Fruit** (*High impact, low effort*)
2. **Simplify Everything** (*what's overly complicated or unnecessary?*)
3. **Make What's Left Better**
4. **Identify & Fill In The Gaps** (*What's missing?*)
5. **Master Maintenance**

Five phases to untangle your business and move it towards sustainability.

Now, while I prefer to see this helpful strategic direction happen in order, the reality is it rarely ever does. In most cases, we're moving along on all five initiatives with one being the primary campaign.

After a few years, we'll eventually get to the final phase, where we master our work and foster a foundation for creating new and better ideas. Once we've completed the process, we'll shift into the IDEMA cycle always moving, never camping out on one stage of the wheel.

Take The Next Step & Move Your Company Forward

You've received a glimpse of what it'll take to level up your company. You must evolve as a leader, grow your team, and improve your revenue-generating systems. It won't be easy, but if you're still a business owner, you let go of *"easy"* years ago.

In many cases, you need a guide to help point the way. You want someone who has been in your shoes, gone through the journey, and actively helps founders through this process.

All the people, tools, insights, and lessons learned from my journey contributed to a system and plan for helping others as they helped me.

By absorbing the previous teaser of each aspect of what it takes to make the jump, the remaining pages in this book will now take you through a deep dive. In each of these sections, we'll explore ideas, stories, and insights to help you embrace the full reality of small business success, and see the actions required for you to make the jump.

By the last page, I want you inspired and equipped to live this out in your life and business.

3. The Five Natural Stages of Every Organization

What if there was a way you could know and predict how your business would unfold? It'd be like the difference in driving across America in the modern-day versus attempting the same trip as the first explorers, Lewis and Clark. While it wouldn't make it easy or prevent all issues, it would certainly provide you a significant advantage.

Shortly after shutting down my marketing company (*of seven years*) in 2014 and exploring my next career opportunities, I was talking with another marketing agency employee about their firm. As they described the company and answered my numerous detailed questions, a sense of deja-vu came over me. I knew where they were at on the journey of their business (*because I had been there*), and the stages that would soon follow.

It reminds me of frog DNA, from Jurassic Park reintroduced in a business context by my friend James Karwisch.

> *"When a company, team, or individual goes about creating a strategy, they like to have as close to a full picture as possible of all the details to give themselves the best chance of heading in the right direction. But what about the times when you don't have a full picture?"* - Jim Karwisch

There are times when we don't have the full understanding, and we infuse our own experiences and perspectives to help us put together a picture of what's going on. That's frog DNA.

Back to my meeting.

I Infused this company's story with the knowledge of my seven-year marketing company's experiences to provide a predictive model for the business journey.

While our company was around for less than a decade, we went through the race quickly, and this expedited pace acted as a catalyst for accelerating my personal development.

As I sat there listening to this person describe the season of their business, I could quickly point to the same moments in my journey, and our progression was strikingly similar.

The mistakes I made on the business journey, the ways I hurt people, and the success I had were all microcosms of what every leader faces. I quickly came to appreciate the opportunity to play in a small sandbox, because I was lucky to fail big in small contexts, unlike those who fail big in highly public ones.

Businesses of all types go through a predictable cycle. Some are larger, slower, and less adaptable, so their journey through the process takes years or decades. Other small companies with learning-oriented leaders are quicker to move through this process. Either way, there is a series of milestones these companies face during their lifetime, and it seems they can be pinpointed and predicted with a useful amount of accuracy.

IDEMA is the framework that best describes this journey. We'll continue to explore it and its business application throughout the book.

When we (*Me, Beth Haun, & Len Wikberg*) first developed IDEMA, we built a project management framework. However, we came to recognize it also applied towards departments and businesses as a whole.

While we briefly surveyed these earlier, let's revisit the five stages born out of desperation to manage our projects by a team of people not inclined towards creating and using structure.

1. **Ideate** - Capture Our Idea.
2. **Discover** - Establish Intentions & Plan To Sustain.
3. **Execute** - Start, Finish, & Prepare To Maintain.
4. **Maintain** - Sustain Our Idea.
5. **Audit** - Determine Our Assessed Idea's Fate.

While these five stages start as a linear process, a company that lasts a lifetime, and even multiple generations, is one that learns to change this process from linear to cyclical.

Here's how these five areas of IDEMA intersect with companies.

#1 - The Ideate Stage - Capture Our Business Ideas

"Where does this invisible table of ideas live?"

My VP of Operations at Noodlehead Marketing was finally fed up with us tabling ideas. This tipping point and the subsequent and consistent form of accountability she imposed on us became part of her way to capture the many ideas we discussed but quickly forgot. Too many great ideas were lost, and she wanted to make sure they were collected and stored with care.

All companies start as an idea. Before we launch our business, we'll have an abundance of ideas we mostly forget. These ideas come and go until one day; we decide to start capturing them. Well, at least one.

This moment is when the idea goes from a fleeting thought to a captured concept. This captured concept is the point where we see the potential and completely ignore the realities that may prevent it from happening. It's also the point where we decide to take ownership of the idea and move it forward, at least to the next discovery step.

Imagine our business idea as a seed to a potentially giant oak tree in our yard. It can be planted to become something great, but if we only collect a jar of seeds, nothing will ever come from them. This lack of action is the downside of the Ideate stage, an abundance of ideas.

The real mission of this stage is to, metaphorically, capture these seeds (*or at least the most important one*) for planting. Moreover, when we do, we can explore them and our intentions further. It's this checkpoint that moves us from the first to the second stage. Discovery.

#2 - The Discover Stage - Establish Intentions & Plan To Sustain The Business

Now that we have a business idea and made the decision to move it forward in the process, now what?

This crossroad moment is the time for research and exploration. What was the origin of the idea? What are the potential payoffs for our customers and us if our idea leads to success? And, what resources do we have to incubate and bring it to life?

These are just a few of the questions we'll explore in the Discover stage. For some, the discovery questions lead to a zealous jump into the next stage. For others, they'll end up asking so many questions they get paralyzed preparing for the jump they'll never actually make.

The critical step in this stage is to take the idea through a deliberate process for determining the viability and feasibility of making this idea work as a business.

Some will have the opportunity for high risk while others will not. The better we plan, the more our intentions and reality will match. However well or poorly designed, we must **make the jump** from planning to execution.

For years, I wanted to launch my company. In retrospect, I was distracted by many other endeavors, some of which I wasn't seeking out. They were opportunistic, chasing the results, but not a way to live out my intentions.

It wasn't until my wife firmly pushed me to start the company that construction on Noodlehead Marketing began.

#3 The Execute Stage - Start, Finish & Prepare To Maintain The Business

We've got an idea, we've thought it out, and now we're going to bring it to life. This stage is where we take the red pill (*from The Matrix*) and move out of the dream world into the real one. But, like a rocket launching into space, this effort requires an abundance of energy to pull off successfully.

Out of excitement and passion, we start erecting our business by finding clients, hiring people, and accumulating resources to help us. In this stage, we can go too far and end up over-committing to more than we can realistically manage well. We say *"yes"* too often, and *"no"* becomes an elusive word.

As we attempt to juggle our company's many conflicting intentions and realities, we end up not doing anything well.

We also find ourselves not sticking around long enough to finish what we start or allow the work to bear fruit. Our impatience leads to chronic abandonment. Often, people pay the price.

The roller coaster of ups and downs is most descriptive of this stage. We're doing great, or we're doing terrible. There is little in between.

Imagine what it was like to ride first class on the titanic eating rich food one moment, and then frantically looking for a lifeboat the moments after hitting the iceberg.

The key to businesses in the execute stage is discipline to finish what was started and not commit to more than we can steward well.

Once we form the habit of completion, the second key is planning to sustain during the finishing leg of each project. **In a world of decay, everything we create requires maintenance. Without sustaining, any success we have will eventually fade away.**

Once our team and we learn the importance of maintenance mastery, we'll migrate our organization into the next stage.

#4 The Maintain Stage - Sustain The Business

Upon entrance to the maintenance stage, we've learned to finish, and we're planning to sustain things we create.

We are pushing the flywheel in a perpetually forward motion. It's like the human body's primary systems (*respiratory, circulatory, nervous, etc.*) running like clockwork. As this continues, the consistency drives growth and benefit to the individual parts of the system as well as the whole.

If you're not sustaining, you're decaying.

Like the human body, a business can't coast on this past success, or it (*like our body*) begins to slowly and unknowingly, get unhealthy. Over time, our organization gets bloated. We keep gaining weight without losing pounds.

Bloated organizations cannot adjust or move as they need to survive & thrive. Eventually, they get caught in the bog, slow down, and fossilize (*just like the dinosaurs*). It's like standing in concrete. Once it's dried, it's almost impossible to move forward.

The key for organizations in this stage is to remember, **we can't always rely on our past success, and anything we maintain needs to be regularly updated; otherwise, it becomes obsolete.**

We also must inject a cadence of review and improvement. We need to shed those pounds and prevent ourselves from ever becoming bloated or fossilized in the first place!

Once we've embraced maintenance, we can now add the last ingredient of **auditing**, our fifth and final stage.

#5 The Audit Stage - Determine Our Assessed Business' Fate

Companies that make it to this stage are almost fully capable of operating in the full IDEMA circle (*if they recognize it*). They're reviewing projects, departments, and people to figure out how to make it all better. If we can't improve it, or justify keeping it as is, it's time to end it.

Keep as-is, improve, or quit?

These are the questions to ask. There are no sacred cows, and everything must have a current justification. With a culture of auditing, we ensure we're as lean and straightforward as possible, while also remaining practical and relevant.

How do we create a real-time feedback loop on all things and people for optimal performance? That is the goal for companies in this stage.

Unfortunately, when we first enter this stage, our company is bloated, so it takes time to shed the fat and get it back to where it needs to be for effective operations.

When we arrive at this high level of performance, we must sustain these review systems to ensure we don't ever go back to building a bloated operation.

The danger in this stage is when we find ourselves auditing so much we don't provide enough time for the changes to take effect (*impatience*). We expect all feedback to lead to instant change. **But, even sound and proven plans executed well often take an extended timeframe to produce positive results** (*patience*).

What Stage Is Your Organization Currently?

If you've owned and operated a company for an extended time, you'll recognize theses stages describe the life cycle of your operation. And, the one you're in now (*or want to arrive at*) is likely the one that resonates most.

When we don't understand this cycle, we traverse through it over and over feeling like we're living out the movie, Groundhog Day with Bill Murray. Every day starts over, and we experience the same things for what seems like forever.

But, when we see and embrace this system, we can proactively engage in it to manage the weaknesses and leverage the strengths.

As you explore the jump in detail, knowing where in the journey your company currently resides, will illuminate insights on how best you can make that upcoming leap, and move your business forward.

4. The JUMP: From Rogue Action Management (*Chaos*) To System Oriented Leadership (*Order*)

Many entrepreneurs thrive creating or operating in chaos. But the adverse effects indicate, this is no way to live and work.

So what is chaotic **rogue action management (RAM)?**

Here's what this problematic management style looks like in the different IDEMA stages.

- New ideas are not captured (*written*).
- Captured ideas are not discovered (*planned*).
- Discovered ideas are not executed (*created*).
- Executed ideas are not maintained (*sustained*).
- Maintained ideas are not audited (*reviewed*).
- Audited ideas are not actioned (*improved*).

Rogue action management (RAM) is merely operating outside of the system's framework. While there are situational moments when rogue management is appropriate (*or even necessary*), we want to name it and minimize the volume of its occurrence.

RAM-ming is no way to build a sustainable business.

New companies will have more of this behavior, but as it matures, there should be a steady decline of rogue action management and an incline of system-oriented leadership. It's vital because toxic and broken issues hide inside the chaos of rogue organizations.

When my life and business were in a tailspin of brokenness, I had a metaphorical vision of myself.

A home.

The house, representing me, was a mess in every section. The rooms were cluttered, the floors stacked with stuff, and the kitchen sink filled with dishes. People were coming in and out, and the music was blaring. Think of the craziest high school party while the parents are away and you'll get a glimpse.

But the cause of the chaos was invisible because of the mess. As I cleaned out this metaphorical house and kept it in working order, I found the source of the disorder. It was a monster living in the basement. It's tentacles extended into and throughout the house, but it wasn't until the house was in order, that I could see the root problem.

Oddly enough, the chaos was a shield, a false sense of safety to hide behind. It's hard because we don't want to look in the mirror. It's more comfortable to sit inside the natural progression towards chaos, and our personalized hell.

So, while we think our issues are external or caused by others, most of them are likely the result of our malice, decisions, lack of boundaries, communication failures, and emotional wounds.

The shift from rogue action management starts with taking responsibility for our part in the chaos and then acting on that ownership to create something better.

Interfaces: How We Work Together

To help us better understand the two dynamics (*chaos and order*) and how they intersect, we'll dive into fast food ordering systems.

The following examples are applicable for two individuals on a team working through a project, two teams within the same organization working on an initiative, or it could also represent two separate companies attempting to work together effectively.

While we can't always control other organizations, usually in a small business you can build an effective, orderly system that even works well with others who are in the midst of chaos (*although there are limitations even for the best run small companies*).

These different partnerships can go well, or they can fail miserably. We'll soon learn the chaos interface has a high cost while the direct interface effectively gets stuff done and grows margin (*which we then apply towards our working relationships*).

Let's start by exploring the worst-case scenario.

The Chaos-To-Chaos Interface

There I was, in the Arby's drive-through lane. My radio was on, and the heater was blasting.

My wife loves Arby's, and I was on a fast-food run to get her Jalapeno Poppers and a Dr. Pepper. As I was ordering, I had a hard time hearing since the intercom was full of static and my car was noisy (*yeah, I should have turned the radio off*).

Regardless, I assumed there was no way they'd get my simple order wrong, but after collecting my to-go bag and driving off, I realized they didn't give me a drink. After driving back to the parking lot, I reviewed my receipt and items. How did I end up with chicken fingers when I ordered a Dr. Pepper and Jalapeno Poppers?

After parking and going inside, we were able to resolve the discrepancy after fifteen minutes.

This messy situation depicts the chaos-to-chaos interface and how it looks when two messy entities attempt to work together.

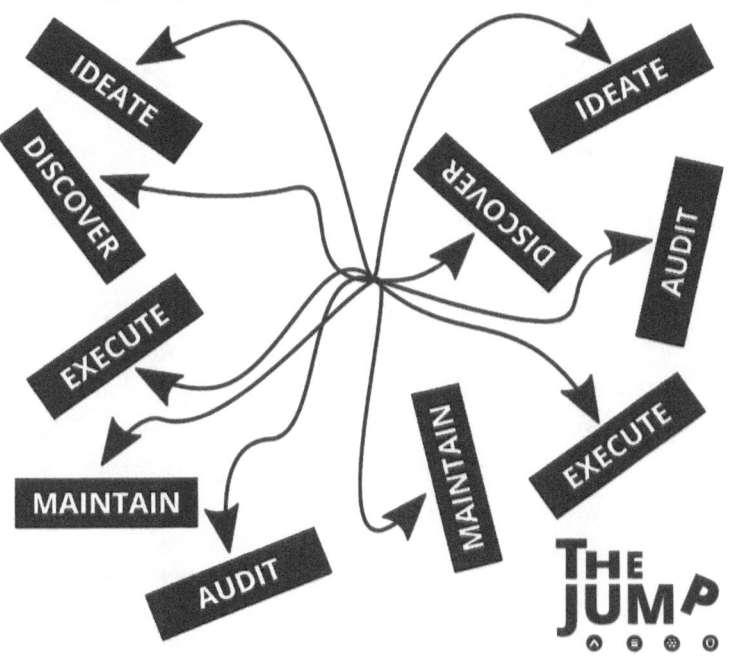

Upon my drive-thru ordering arrival, I was in chaos with loud noises. Unbeknownst to me, the store had their chaos in taking the order with a broken intercom system. For us both to get what we wanted out of the situation, it required additional effort, time, and clarity as we sorted through the tangled mess. With higher stakes, the consequences are dire.

All of this disarray could have been avoided if one or both of us operated in an effective and orderly manner.

Like using a credit card with interest accruing (*because you don't pay it off right away*) instead of paying the full amount upfront with cash, the disorder has a higher and preventable cost.

When we're not intentional while working with others, the chaos interface is the natural choice. Useful outcomes are the result of sheer luck or the intentionality of someone else.

The Filter Interface: Chaos-To-Order

If you've managed your business or worked with vendors as I've described, you'll want to seek a better way to operate. Ideally, you'll want an intentional orderly system, like Chick-Fil-A. This well run organization has excellent food, service, and an underappreciated ordering process.

My go-to item is the Spicy Chicken Sandwich with pepper jack and no pickles. After asking me if I want the meal or just the sandwich, I'll request the meal. I'll respond to their request for a drink by ordering a Coke. In response to them asking me if I want any condiments, I'll ask for buffalo sauce. They repeat my order back to me, inform me of my order's cost, and I proceed towards the payment window after confirming.

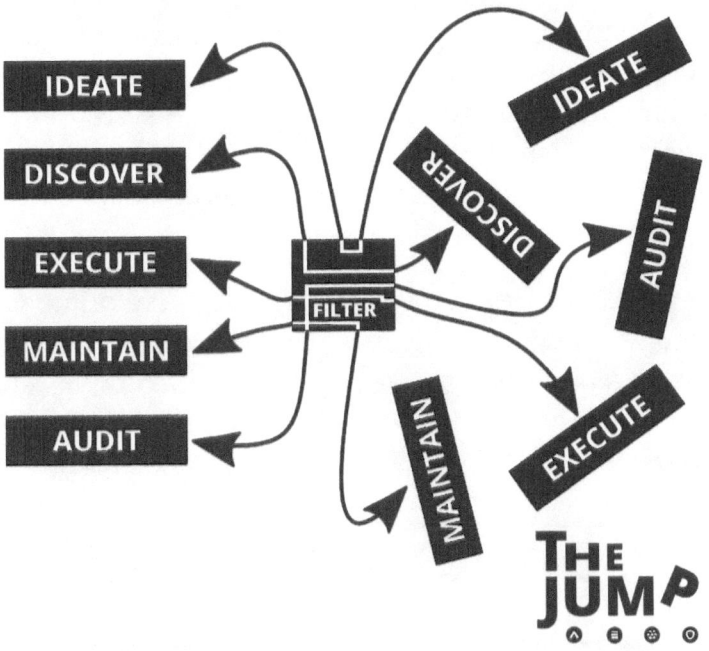

Chick-Fil-A has a process, and regardless of my awareness or understanding of it, they lead me through it. They take me from my temporary state of chaos and put me into their state of order.

In this transition, I choose to yield to their ordering process for a short amount of time, so I can get my food (*but it doesn't mean I understand or appreciate it*). The filter interface is where one party has an orderly system, and they lead a guest through it.

The Direct Interface: Order²

After shopping Chick-Fil-A regularly, I've learned their process. I know how they're going to take my order, and it allows me to give them the results their system expects proactively. Knowing this, I operate within their steps for a mutually beneficial and expedient engagement.

Now when I order at the window, I request a number three with pepper jack cheese and no pickle. Please make it a meal with a coke, and add buffalo sauce. That will be all for my order. I say, *"thank you,"* and they say *"my pleasure."* I drive towards the payment window.

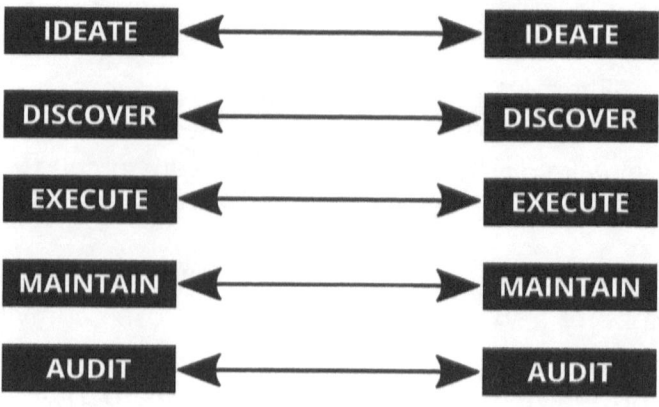

The direct interface is when both parties are using the same process and definitions of words (*language*). When we operate in the direct interface, we're exponentially more productive and efficient as a result of eliminating waste.

The beauty of this productivity is not just the time we save, but the time we can now use in building relationships with our team and clients.

Let's be more productive at our work so we can have more margin, and give others more time.

As you hear me describe three stories, which interface scenario is most like the inside of your business operations (*between people, teams, and departments*)? How do you work with your customers? And your vendors?

I suspect if you're reading this book, it's not the direct interface. So, the question begs, how do you change from operating within a chaotic state?

How do you make, the jump?

What Is *"The JUMP"*?

> *"What got you here, won't get you there."* - Marshall Goldsmith

The Jump is going from chaos to order. It's transitioning from rogue (*RAM*) to system-oriented leadership (*SOL*), where we migrate from the chaos to the direct interface (*at least internally*). It's also when you stop leveraging your authority as the business owner to RAM things through the business and start using your influence instead.

> *"Instead of craving control, in complexity we have to shift thinking about influence. We will not be able to make things happen, but we can be thoughtful about how we support the emergence of the things we want."* - Jennifer Garvey Berger, Unlocking Leadership Mindtraps

The Jump is the transition of intentionally designing your operations and communications for successfully arriving at the company vision (*and your personal vision too*). You will match your behavior to your intentions by embracing reality and maintaining a sustainable business. You will follow through on your design to its completion.

Unfortunately, business owners are successfully growing their company through a chaotic state, and they don't have the knowledge, experience, or maturity to change how they operate. It feels wrong because their approach got them this far, why abandon it now?

It reminds me of Tiger Woods.[2] Shortly after winning the Masters in April 1997, Tiger Woods decided to tear his technique apart and build it from the ground up. He'd reinvent his golf swing two more times in 2004 (*which he'd follow with six championships through 2008*), and 2010 (*which led to an extended season of drought due to his personal moral failures*). After 11 years, he'd go on to win the Masters in 2019.

---

[2] Eden, Scott: "Stroke of madness." *ESPN*, ESPN Enterprises, Inc. 22 Jan, 2013, espn.com/golf/story/_/id/8865487/

What Woods recognized was his way couldn't get him across the chasm. For him, his aspiration for greatness pulled him to elevate his game. For others, it's not until they're sick and tired of being *"sick and tired"* that change begins to happen.

We have to choose to change, and to recognize our approach worked this far, but its limits will prevent us from creating the type of business we desire. For me, the shift required a moment of growth and forced a change in me to understand a new and better way to operate.

Learning A New Way

In 2013, the entire team at Noodlehead Marketing took a year to rest and reflect on our journey. This sabbath year (*I'll explain later in this chapter*) was a large part of me learning how to bridge the gap.

One breakthrough came when I learned how to practically translate the IDEMA system into our family life as a way for us to get organized and focused. However, it wasn't as direct as I had used in the business.

My wife was not interested in using or going through any of my IDEMA processes, so I was forced to set aside my way of collecting ideas, and processing them (*discussing and planning*) to resolve our chaotic family situation. I had to find another way of application to get the benefit while also meeting my wife where she was.

With a third child on the way, she was exhausted caring for the house, kids, and her community responsibilities. She didn't have the time to muster the necessary interest to both learn and apply my newfound processes that had helped so much in my business.

But, I still wanted to help alleviate the pain and bring order to the chaos while better understanding her role in the family, and by leveraging my strengths and tools.

After she quickly fell into a feeling of despair, that there was no way out of this cycle of chaos, I got busy surveying our context and assertively finding ways to help. I dug in so I could apply my processes as an intuitive partner (*without her explicit input*).

This effort involved getting up early with the kids, letting her sleep in, making breakfast, and doing chores around the house. Due to the challenges during the pregnancy of our third child, the doctor placed her on bed rest for an extended period. And during it, I continued to keep the household running well.

While doing tasks, I wrote the actions required for our house to run smoothly, and also grouped them into manageable categories for reflection, improvement, and consistency.

The Epiphany

Before this revelation, my approach with ideas was to capture, discover, build, and then maintain them (*which was a reinvention from how I operated at the chaotic start of the business*).

In this situation, I had to assess the situation quickly and identify where I could help. Each day I'd find ways to support, and eventually, I was able to alleviate enough pressure to establish a comfortable margin for my wife and me. It also allowed me to objectively discover how we could manage it all better (*and my grocery inventory system was quite impressive*).

IDEMA is limited in how it can help us in a state of chaos, but this new series of lessons learned allowed me to morph the system in a practically beneficial way.

In a crazy state, we need someone who can transition (*or translate*) us towards a system such as IDEMA as a way of helping us out of the chaos and towards sustainable business management. We can't do it alone, and many times, we don't know how to ask or get the help that will truly make a difference.

Business owners need help capturing the rogue activities and getting them done, so things don't get worse. They need help organizing these actions to begin properly discovering them. They need help establishing clarity, so they don't perpetually stay stuck.

But it gets messy. It's as if we have crashed a fully stocked vehicle in a mud trench. There is not a clear and easy process to get back on the road. We need to help pull each other out and grab the cargo worth salvaging. Once we get out of the trench (*chaos*) and onto the road (*order*), we can make real progress.

The Chaos To Order Journey Requires Two Initiatives

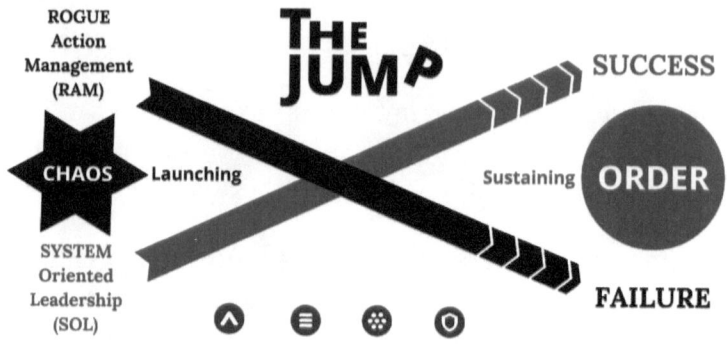

To exit this operational habit of rogue management requires two active initiatives. Minimize rogue action management (RAM) and maximize system-oriented leadership (*SOL*)

Rogue action management (*RAM*), the first effort, includes the things we feel need to get done to move the organization forward. To begin the minimization, we'll want to establish accountability and create scheduled follow up to ensure we're effectively transitioning into sustainable proactive systems.

The second campaign is where we capture and process new ideas through the IDEMA framework (*or something comparable*). We want to discover and execute them properly. We want to ensure we are maintaining with excellence. We want to schedule a time when we regularly audit ourselves to ensure we are going in the right direction.

Over time we'll operate system-centric and seldom as rogue agents. This transition describes the journey, one where we minimize chaos and create order.

When people within the order ecosystem are not bottlenecks, this system empowers people to more effectively do what they do best. It allows them to thrive, and the community to flourish.

With rogue action management, we have an abundance of autonomy, and it's unpleasant giving it up. **Until you see the value of working as a team, communicating the same language, and ultimately delegating your authority to others, you won't make the jump.**

That is why to leap requires *you look in the mirror* and recognize *you must change* to foster the development of the company *you seek to create.*

The mission depends on it.

The Four Steps To Transform Your Business From Chaos To Clarity

> *"You have been down there, Neo. You know that road. You know exactly where it ends. And I know that's not where you want to be."* Trinity, The Matrix [3]

---

[3] The Matrix. Dir. Lilly and Lana Wachowski. Perf. Carrie-Anne Moss. Warner Brothers, 1999. DVD.

When we feel stuck in our small business, it's a great time to reflect on the journey and where to go next. No owner wants a stalling small business. We want a company that continues to grow and thrive. But when that no longer happens, we wonder what we should do next when everything we try perpetuates our wheel spinning.

You've got three options for how to move forward from here. You can keep going as-is, hoping things will change on their own (*they won't*). You can make foundational changes to orient the company how you want, or lastly, you can shut the business down (*or sell it*) and move on.

Same. Change. End.

Running the business the same way as you have is merely going to bring you back to this point.

You've been there. You know where that leads.

Eventually, you won't be able to kick the can down the road, and you'll have to make a move. So, unless you suddenly become content with the business you have, the second and third options are the paths to explore.

Do you **change** the business or bring it to its **conclusion** (*selling or shutting down*)?

In my journey, I experienced the challenge of facing them both. And, when you own your company long enough, you will too.

After years of being shaped by the external forces of friends, family, clients, and staff, I began asking myself how I'd run my marketing agency if I were to start it again from scratch. What would an intentional marketing agency look like now that I've learned a great deal from the experience?

A few years later, after becoming that intentional organization, I began exploring what I'd vocationally do if I could start over and choose anything, or any business.

> **Key Questions**
> - If you were to start your business over from scratch, what would you do differently? How would you structure and run it?
> - If you could start over vocationally and do anything you wanted, would it be running the business you currently own?

Obvious to me now is how the last question should have been the one I answered before ever launching the company. Yep, I had it backward, and so do most young entrepreneurs.

While navigating this decision, it was helpful for me to understand what was required and the change necessary to effectively make the jump to a sustainable and growing small business. What's next is going to be hard, so is this business or something else what I want?

Four Required Steps For Making The Jump

As you consider leaping to a new and better business, here are the four steps you'll need to take before jumping. We'll explore further in the subsequent chapters, but here's a quick survey of what's required to thrive in your upgraded small business.

1. Level Up As A Person & Leader

When your small business is stuck, it's because you are in the way. Instead of a conduit, you're a bottleneck. Moreover, the only way for your business to become what you want it to be is for you to get out of the way and become a self-authored (*more details on this later*) and internally driven leader.

This level up action requires looking in the mirror, reflecting on the past, defining the desired future, and living in a way that brings the vision to life daily.

The good news is, we will lean into adult development theory to provide you a map on how to effectively mature and grow as a person. With the help of scientific discovery, you'll face your fears, explore your complaints, and dive into what you value most.

When you're willing to do the hard work of authentically knowing yourself and making the necessary changes to accelerate your growth, you'll be ready for the jump.

2. Build Strong Business Foundations

Making the jump with a strong foundation means defining where it is your jump will take you. While your business can be fun, it's not just about having a good time. It requires a mission and clarity on where that takes us.

For you visionaries, it means choosing one path when there are unlimited pathways in front of us (*a definition of strategy*). Keeping our options open leads us to quickly tangle ourselves up, preventing us from ever going down a single path in a deep and meaningful way.

If you're ready to articulate your intentions and set a definite destination, you'll be prepared to make that jump.

3. Guide & Filter Your Loyal Team

Internally, we change. From it, we set the stage for the business. The subsequent test is engaging our team with clear direction. Some will love it; others will actively resist it, and resist you. You'll no longer enjoy the comfort of appeasing employees and clients because with a clear vision, some will feel excluded, and you'll cause others to leave.

But, you'll also get further buy-in from those dedicated to the vision and you as the leader to get them there. They'll be your essential core.

When you're ready to let go of the fear of missing out, and invite only those who are genuinely committed to the end game (*which you've clearly defined*), you'll be ready to move from this third step to the fourth and final one.

4. Leverage Sustainable Systems & Modeled Mindsets

With a strong foundation, an effective leader, and a loyal team, the key now is gluing these pieces together with a modeled mindset and sustainable systems.

What's the culture and processes required to achieve a high level of success? How do we maximize our strengths while effectively managing our weaknesses? How do we build something beyond any one of us, where all of us are simply a small piece of a significant and meaningful puzzle?

Are we practiced in living a disciplined life (*words aren't enough*) that makes it possible for us to move the needle, embrace reality, and make the vision real?

For those ready to accept this fourth challenge, they're prepared to take the last step before making the jump.

Planning Your Next Steps

This is your glimpse, into the reality of what's required for your business to be what you always wanted, and what you hoped could be the reality.

Are you willing to dive deep in these four areas? Will it be worth it, in the end? Alternatively, should you end it now and make the jump with something else?

Deciding on whether to end a business venture is no easy task, but if you wanted easy, you wouldn't have chosen entrepreneurship.

My story in the following sections will provide other angles for you to explore this tension and decide your destiny.

How To Decide Whether Or Not To End a Business Venture

No matter how well organized and self-directed your organization (*or project*) may be, it indeed does require a vision-centric leader to move it forward. If you thought you could launch something and have it lead itself, I'm sorry to say that type of business is quite rare (*if not impossible*).

Hopefully, you recognize this and take the time to intentionally decide what happens next with your organization that currently hangs in the balance of your decision.

Let's start with a question.

Does it make more sense to change and continue or to stop and shut down?

As you think through how to answer that question, let me share several stories of when I've ended or pivoted along a journey to inspire you towards your most appropriate, and likely hard, next step.

I. I'm Learning, But This Venture Is Not Fruitful

Before Christmas 2005, a talk radio show host commented about how every time someone says *"Happy Holidays"* instead of *"Merry Christmas"* an elf dies. It sparked an idea to launch a satirical website running with this theme called *Save An Elf*. After calling into several political news shows and getting interviewed about the site's creative images and elf death counter, the website received tens of thousands of visitors.

It was a huge success. Afterward, my wife suggested a spin-off idea where I would take the concept and apply it in a more meaningful way. Subsequently, I launched *SaveTheSoldiers.com*, a political news website aimed at supporting the armed forces. We would call out those using soldiers as a political football and would showcase soldiers and their perspective on the site.

In early 2006, I launched this digital platform and spent an enormous amount of time without earning an income. While I had a decent amount of online success and learned internet marketing, this major side project wasn't sustainable.

I was highly encouraged by my wife to either find a way to make money at it or launch Noodlehead Marketing. I chose the latter and used my previous production skills with my newfound marketing abilities to launch a marketing agency.

As you read my story about a time-consuming and unprofitable venture, does your business come to mind? Are you investing a large amount of your time with little or no return? Is it time for you to let it go, and move on?

II. The Way I'm Running The Company Is Not Working

Several years into launching my marketing company, I reached a half-time moment. If I were to start a marketing company from scratch, what would that company look like, and how would I build it?

We had become a fulfillment organization creating what was asked of us (*videos, websites, email campaigns, etc.*) only to face disappointed customers when projects were complete (*If we build it, they will come. So they thought*).

While we were fulfilling the work, they unrealistically expected their project to deliver specific results. They also didn't communicate these expectations, and we didn't know to ask poignant questions on the front end.

What we came to recognize is that these projects required a strategic direction. Much like an arrow needs a bow to move through the air and an archer to hit the target, so do tactical marketing initiatives need a strategy.

And, these companies needed a grounded foundation of purpose (*why?*) and direction (*vision*), not just project direction.

Learning these lessons and facing the question of what a new marketing company would look like, I decided to push forward and build upon this new understanding.

It reminds me of the parable of the farmer and the fig tree (*a story we'll revisit*). The owner wanted to cut down the tree because it wasn't bearing the desired fruit. The farmer protested asking for a year to set the tree up for success. If after special care it still didn't produce fruit, he'd cut it down.

As we see with the farmer, I saw the potential of rebooting the company in a new and better way. It was hard to transition, but it was well worth the challenge.

So, my next question for you is the one I sought to answer for myself. If you were to start your business from scratch today, what would you do differently? What would be different about that company compared to the one you have now?

III. Scaling Back a Project That Failed To Launch

In 2014, I formally shut down my marketing company only to immediately become a freelancer when my business and marketing services were sought out by those in my network. Eight months later, this incoming stream of prospects never ended, and I embraced the life of a full-time freelancer. After a year of mastering the vocation, freelancers sought me out for advice. This journey led to writing and publishing my first book, *Path of the Freelancer: An Actionable Guide to Flourishing in Freelancing.*

With as many resources as I could give it, while also maintaining my primary source of income, I launched and promoted the book. There were several interviews and speaking events, but it was not enough momentum to move the project to an ongoing sustainable venture. So, I had a choice. Grow Path of the Freelancer's digital footprint or my personal brand's platform.

Growing my digital footprint would have a stronger long-term impact. By blogging on my website, I'm building up my current consulting services while also working on improving my abilities, experiences, and knowledge to more effectively execute on the needs of my paying customers.

So, I deepened my focus on my personal blog and transformed the Path of the Freelancer website to a static online resource. It's a vast repository for freelancers as it is, but the website now rarely changes. This update resulted in reworking the menu, updating language, and making it simpler to buy the book.

In minimal maintenance mode, it requires almost none of my time. I now only pay for hosting and the domain name.

In this case, the book and complementary resources are tremendously valuable, so it's worth keeping it published.

I've also published two other resources that came from the marketing company journey.

Both IDEMA and The Island Story were published online for others to explore. I reference and share them both in my work and human interactions.

These were all worth publishing in minimal maintenance mode. And, the same may be true for your venture.

IV. This Business Is Not The Path For Me

After we shifted gears in the marketing business, we changed our company to a living representation of our vision (*intentional companies reflecting excellence*).

Some team members came with us willingly, while others left on their own accord. Others required firing as new people joined the crew.

At the end of 2012, I looked around at our prosperous clients, great team, and the meaningful work we were doing and was mostly satisfied. We had arrived at the destination. With this arrival came a sense of finality. The mission was complete, so now what?

In prayer, I sought an answer. To make a long story short, we decided as a company to take a sabbath year (*more details later in the chapter*). We would not seek out new business and would take a year to rest and reflect. The result would either lead to continuing the company or ending it. Halfway through the year, I was compelled to conclude the business, shutting it down March 31st, 2014.

While it wasn't as clear to me at the moment, one pivotal question that I had to answer was the following one.

If I were to start over vocationally, would I choose to create and sustain a marketing company for the remainder of my working life?

As the creator and founder of something, it's helpful for us to dive deep into the origin of why we launched the idea. By doing so, we'll discover that we began it to accomplish a personal objective.

For me, the marketing company was my way of taking control of my destiny. I thought it would be a vehicle to help me become a movie director. Not only did that not happen, but it also moved me further away from this path. At this moment in my life, I realized it was time to backtrack to where I started and go a different way.

What about you? If you had complete freedom to choose a vocational path, would it be the one you're on? Would it involve the business you're currently running?

Pulling All The Pieces Together Into a Focused Series of Questions

I've been through the process of auditing my company and side venture intentions on many occasions with a variety of conclusions. While I share these stories to inspire and help you on your journey, the reality is that each situation is uniquely different and will require you to spend time answering the hard questions.

You need to know your personal motivations. This understanding will help you see how this business venture is contributing to moving you toward the finish line.

Below, I've compiled the key questions for this audit. As you read through them, take the time to write down your answers so you can explore the future of your endeavor.

> **Key Questions**
>
> - What's your personal objective?
> - How does this venture contribute or distract from it?
> - How is this project contributing to your long-term goals (*aspirations*) and your short-term needs (*paying the bills*)?
> - If you were to start this venture over again, would you do things differently? How would that look?
> - If you were to start over vocationally, would you choose the path you're on? If your answer is no, does a change in vocation mean shutting down, selling or pivoting?
> - Utility: Is this venture providing a solution to a problem? How unique is this solution compared to alternatives?
> - Viability: Is there a realistic, profitable path to success?

- If you're going to continue the venture, do you need to change how you're doing it, or scale it back?
- If you're going to shut it down, would it be fruitful for you and others to write about and share the stories and lessons learned as a public memorial?

With clarity on why you're going down the path you're on, the results that you expect to find at the end of that path, and an understanding of how this venture helps accelerate or make the journey possible, it'll become quite clear if you need to continue as is, change how you're going about it, or stop it altogether.

If you're not sure what to do next, or how to even process how to proceed with your business, I've got an unconventional way you can explore the fate of your small business.

A Sabbath year.

A Release Process For Deliberating On Your Small Business' Fate

What would it look like if your business took an entire year off? Is it possible or crazy? What would be the fruit of this endeavor?

In 2013, the entire Noodlehead Marketing team embraced a whole year of rest and release, a Sabbath

Year (*Shmita in Hebrew*). At the time, I never heard of an organization taking a sabbatical (*just individuals*) and after extensive research to find an example, that didn't change.

As we explored taking a year off for the company, we were limited to trusting God and the few scriptures he left on the topic to discover what it was and how to apply them to our upcoming year.

Once we committed, there was a roller coaster of wonderful and scary moments. In retrospect, it was critical in instilling values and changes in me, my marriage, and elsewhere. And, it gave me what I needed to make the jump.

So while it may feel quite risky to do, taking a Sabbath year could be the best thing you ever do. It was for me.

What Is a Sabbath Year?

Every seven years, the Israelites (*from the Hebrew Scriptures*) would allow the farmland to rest. During this time, they could live off of what crops the land produced, but the people were not to stockpile anything that grew from it.

Here's how Leviticus chapter twenty-five explains the Sabbath year.

> "When you enter the land I am going to give you, the land itself must observe a Sabbath to the Lord. For six years sow your fields, and for six years prune your vineyards and gather their crops. But in the seventh year, the land is to have a year of

Sabbath rest, a Sabbath to the Lord. **Do not sow your fields or prune your vineyards. Do not reap what grows of itself or harvest the grapes of your untended vines.** *The land is to have a year of rest. Whatever the land yields during the Sabbath year will be food for you—for yourself, your male and female servants, and the hired worker and temporary resident who live among you, as well as for your livestock and the wild animals in your land. Whatever the land produces may be eaten."*

The intent behind the Sabbath Year was to place a pause button in Jewish society so people could focus on what mattered most. God, their family, and community. Unfortunately for the Israelites, they mostly failed to honor this directive. They eventually fell into captivity for seventy years, which was the number of Sabbath years they failed to follow.

When we don't take time to rest, we're eventually forced to do so. One such example is when I worked crazy hours every day and all the time. Finally, my body broke down, and I got sick for a week.

We can't escape rest.

Research also shows that while we can get a boost of productivity from working more than forty-hour-weeks, we face diminishing returns when working long hours over extended periods.[4] We're most productive, consistently over time, when we maintain a forty-hour workweek.

---

[4] Robinson, Evan: "Why Crunch Modes Doesn't Work: Six Lessons." IGDA, 2005, www.igda.org/page/crunchsixlessons

It sounds to me a bit like the story of the tortoise and the hare.

Why Our Company & Team Took A Sabbath Year

Since we're not Jewish, how in the world did we end up taking a Sabbath year? And, what does that even mean in the modern era?

Let me explain.

In 2010 during the half-time of Noodlehead Marketing, I asked, what if I were to start a marketing company from scratch, knowing what I know and learning the lessons I learned? How would I do it differently now compared to when I started?

After answering this question, and over the subsequent years, we transformed the company into this newfound vision (*Intentional Companies Reflecting Excellence*). In 2011, we became the *intentional organization reflecting excellence*.

In 2012, we experienced the many fruits of this labor. Our team was amazing, our clients were great, the work we did was meaningful, and we were making money.

As the year progressed, I felt a strong sense of completion. We had set out to change our company and help others in the same way. And we did it. Now what?

My prayer shifted. Were we to continue our mission, serving clients how we were or was it time to end what we created and set off on a new adventure? What was next on my professional journey as well as the team?

Seeking an answer from God led to a compelling urge to talk with my wife (*who had exited the business years before*) about the future of Noodlehead Marketing.

For the previous year, she was studying the Sabbath year, although entirely unrelated to the business. After thinking and praying about it, she felt compelled to share the Sabbath passage and remind me that Noodlehead Marketing was entering its seventh year (*2013-2014*). Concluding our discussion, we agreed that we would take the business through a Sabbath year.

However, we had no idea what this meant. The passage was talking about land and farming, both of which we didn't have. As Christians, we don't adhere to the Jewish Scriptures. (*we reference it for history, inspiration, and principles*)

We had to dig deeper to get direction from the underlying principles.

The Hebrew word used for Sabbath Year is Shmita, and it means **to release or to let go**. This meaning was our starting point and your key for making the jump.

So, how would this practically apply to the business? I studied the available scriptures, shared with the team, and we explored the verses together.

Unsure how they'd respond (*because of their different worldviews*), I was surprised when all three other team members agreed to embrace the plan. One found merit in the practical benefits while the other wanted a front-row seat to what was going to happen (*bring the popcorn!*). The third trusted me and embraced the value of our leap of faith.

With all four of us on board, we took time to decide why we're doing this, what we hoped to accomplish, the mission, and guidelines we'd follow through the process. These were our Sabbath year intentions. From this grounded foundation, we extracted six principles we'd follow throughout the year.

If you're not sure about your company's future, these Sabbath Year principles provide a framework for you to follow for a period of three, six, or twelve months to reflect on your journey thus far, and discover a decision for how you'll move forward.

Our Sabbath Year Intentions

Leveraging the elements from the Formula For Intentionality (*details in chapter seven*), we went into the Sabbath year with particular intentions defining each aspect of our objectives and how we'd approach the process.

Here's what we concluded.
- **Why were we doing it?** To trust God for provision.
- **What was our vision? What would we deem as a success after the Sabbath year?** Individual Noodleheads lived into their personal visions (a *springboard to what's next, regardless of what it was*).
- **Our Mission:** Resting in what's provided.

Guiding Values

- **Graceful** in the understanding of Jewish law.
- Spouses are **brought along** and **are part** of the financial threshold discussion (*we would not persist if our spouse chose to stop participating*).
- We operate with set **margins** (*time & treasures*).
- **Listening** and **being still**.
- **Celebrate** all blessing.
- Only **share when invited**.
- We will **hold our heads high**.

Specific Principles Inspired From The Scriptures

While there are guidelines and directions for how to take a Sabbath year in the Bible, the details were quite sparse. Since we didn't have physical land and crops, we embraced the principles and adapted them to our context. It was a profound exercise transcending its original application.

The following six principles illuminate the scripture references and how we interpreted and applied them during the Sabbath year.

1. **Fields & Vineyards** (*Don't launch new things or review and make what already exists better*)
2. **Not Storing Up** (*Operate as a conduit. What comes in, goes out*)
3. **Releasing of Slaves** (*Bring loyal outsiders into the fold*)

4. **Community Support** (*We receive help from those who offer it*)
5. **Debt Forgiveness**
6. **We Will Rest, Operate With Margin, & Give**

The process of discovering these intentions, and the principles involved, allowed each of us to contribute specific elements resulting in a powerful combination. This strong foundation gave clear directives and guidance for when it became challenging during the year.

Let's explore each of these insights individually. When contrasted with the idea of striving for success, they each provide sharp insight into the struggle I faced as an entrepreneur, and wisdom for the jump to come.

Principle 1: Fields & Vineyards

> *"...but during the seventh year, the land must have a Sabbath year of complete rest. It is the Lord's Sabbath. Do not plant your fields or prune your vineyards during that year." - Leviticus 25:4*

This directive was our reference scripture for the first principle.

We concluded from it; we would **restrain ourselves from discovering new ideas** (*do not plant your fields*) for the business. We would also **restrain ourselves from auditing existing projects and business structure** (*or prune your vineyards*) to make things better.

We were continually launching new ideas and evaluating, so this task was not easy. At first, we caught ourselves doing this anyway! Slowly and surely, we moved towards the vision and operated within these guidelines.

Also, while we were a marketing agency, we would **refrain from seeking out new project fulfillment work**, but we would accept incoming projects where our services were explicitly requested.

We also chose **not to audit any existing partnerships** and instead would maintain the ones we had how we had them.

At the offset of the Sabbath year, work picked up, and we made more money than usual.

When it dipped back down a few months in, it was challenging to refrain from seeking new paying projects (*sales*).

It also required I learn that while the company would contribute to the provision of the team, I was not their sole provider (*God is*).

Throughout the Sabbath year, we had past clients unexpectedly reaching out to us (*without any prodding*) about helping with a variety of projects.

The provision came; it just didn't always come in the ways we expected.

How would your business change if you didn't act on any new ideas for a year? If you sat with how things were without making them better? Alternatively, you didn't market for new business and instead worked on what was in front of you?

If these are habitual negative behaviors in your organization, like they were with us, it's transformational.

Principle 2: Not Storing Up

> "And don't store away the crops that grow on their own or gather the grapes from your unpruned vines. The land must have a year of complete rest. But you may eat whatever the land produces on its own during its Sabbath. This applies to you, your male and female servants, your hired workers, and the temporary residents who live with you." - Leviticus 25:5-6

All income generated during the Sabbath year would be used to pay us employees and other financial obligations (*expenses*).

Based on our salaries, we gave a percentage weight to each of us on the team. Whatever money was in the bank was distributed based on this percentage (*a built-in dividend return*). When the company made more money, we received a larger paycheck. When we earned less, our paychecks were smaller (*as was our time working*).

The business would not accumulate any funds. What came in went out to the team. Since our expenses were minimal, most of the income was distributed based on our salary weighting (*which could quickly get complicated with a larger organization*).

In this step of faith, we learned what happens when we stepped back and expected God to step forward.

Principle 3: Releasing of Slaves

> *"...this is what the Lord, the God of Israel, says: I made a covenant with your ancestors long ago when I rescued them from their slavery in Egypt. I told them that every Hebrew slave must be freed after serving six years..." - Jeremiah 34:12*

With this seemingly irrelevant passage (*in a modern American context*), we actually thought of a relevant application.

There was a contractor who was working with Noodlehead Marketing, and we decided to commit to him as an employee with a set salary (*knowing the workload would likely decrease*).

To us, this was an act of bringing him into the fold as one of us (*the intention behind the directive*), while also trusting God would provide when we were fearful that he would not.

If you suspect or know there are people that feel trapped within your organization, explore how you could help set them free. It could come from changing their situation, their role, or the organization they're employed by (*yours*).

Principle 4: Community Support

> *"...take a sacred offering for the Lord. Let those with generous hearts present the following gifts to the*

Lord (See 6-20)…..So the whole community of Israel left Moses and returned to their tents. All whose hearts were stirred and whose spirits were moved came and brought their sacred offerings to the Lord. They brought all the materials needed for the Tabernacle, for the performance of its rituals, and for the sacred garments. Both men and women came, all whose hearts were willing. They brought to the Lord their offerings of gold—brooches, earrings, rings from their fingers, and necklaces. They presented gold objects of every kind as a special offering to the Lord." - Exodus 35:4-5,20-22

In response to this passage, we committed to remaining open to receiving help from those who were compelled to help us individually and collectively. We experienced an abundance of community generosity from food and Christmas presents to a minivan. It was transformational to receive so much based not on merit, but the loving kindness of others.

Within this principle of community support, we also chose the following guidelines:

- We would keep a list of our collective needs, updated as they changed.
- We would communicate the needs, to family members of the Noodleheads.
- We decided individually if we communicated the needs to anyone outside of the team members and their spouse.
- We would bring our spouses along in the Sabbath Year commitment process.

Before going into the Sabbath year, we all met together with our spouses (*as a group*) to explore our intent and these principles. We worked through the concerns and anticipations. We would not move forward unless we were all on board to do so.

Thankfully, we all were committed to the journey and subsequently commenced at the beginning of our seventh year. Throughout it, we shared, helped each other, and embraced the help of our communities in different ways.

We learned to receive freely.

Principle 5: Debt Forgiveness

> *"At the end of every seventh year, you must cancel the debts of everyone who owes you money. This is how it must be done. Everyone must cancel the loans they have made to their fellow Israelites. They must not demand payment from their neighbors or relatives, for the Lord's time of release has arrived."*
> *- Deuteronomy 15:1-2*

In response to this scripture, we chose to forgive all financial debts owed to us by clients once the Sabbath year concluded. We proactively reached out to clients who owed money to inform them of their debt forgiveness. Some embraced the debt forgiveness while others pushed back declining it, which was unexpected.

We also chose to forgive all those with emotional and spiritual debt. During the year, we reflected, noted, and followed up on all opportunities for us to proactively reconcile with others.

It is a powerful and challenging activity when we let go of something legitimately owed to us.

Principle 6: We Will Rest, Operate With Margin, & Give

> *"...but during the seventh year, the land must have a Sabbath year of complete rest. It is the Lord's Sabbath." - Leviticus 25:4*

In the years preceding the Sabbath, I pushed for margin in my life, family, community, and work. We laid the groundwork, and the subsequent journey would be a practice to sustain the mindset and habits when the challenges increased.

Knowing we would have an abundance of time on our hands during the Sabbath year, we needed to predetermine how we would steward it. The following guidelines gave us clarity.

- We operated with a 20% time margin commitment. **We considered 80% at full capacity.**
- When we had extra time (*because work was limited*), we processed it in the following order.
    - Complete existing internal projects under our responsibility.
    - Help team members complete their internal projects.
    - Rest, pray, worship, and study God's word.

- Give time to our families and our communities.
- Give time to clients and those we knew through the business.

For my family, this margin ended up being critical. Several months into the Sabbath year, my wife went on bedrest during our third child's pregnancy (*mentioned earlier*). With my extra time, I took over managing household responsibilities, including preparing meals, cleaning, groceries, and caring for the kids.

Without a slowdown in the Sabbath year, I'm not sure how we would have adapted to this unexpected turn of events.

The embrace of resting while acting generous has a powerful way of teaching us the principle of margin.

Reflecting On These Intentions, Principles, & The Sabbath Year Experience

The journey through this twelve-month experience hard-coded these values in me. I trace much of my freelancing success back to the different elements from the Sabbath year. Many of which I failed to overcome before it. Now, many of these disciplines are second nature, as I seek to live the Sabbath as a lifestyle.

The Sabbath year was a powerful experience for us, collectively and individually. The first half, for me, felt like being on the mountaintop with God (*experiencing numerous miracles*), while the second half felt like walking through the valley of death (*the most challenging season of my life*).

Through the journey, we all hoped it would lead to relaunching Noodlehead Marketing, but unfortunately, halfway through I decided to let go of the company and move in a different direction vocationally.

The experience was a launching pad for the four of us Noodleheads to go in four different directions, as we had originally understood.

For me, this decision to shut down the company felt like a death, and the emotions hit me like a semi-truck. Through this tragedy, I experienced God's grace in new and more profound ways.

Through the entire year, He developed my character and healed me from the wounds of my journey.

While the company concluded, it launched me unexpectedly into freelancing (*and consulting*) full-time, which continues to this day.

This entrepreneurial experiment resulted in deeply anchored lessons, insights, and disciplines.

In this way, Noodlehead Marketing was my cocoon, and the journey after was embracing the new transformed version of me (*as the butterfly*).

When I find myself striving for something unsuccessfully, I need to audit my intent and behavior to explore why. **The Sabbath (*rest*) is an unexpected antidote to this striving state.**

This section only scratches the surface of the journey. With such a rich experience, I could write a book about it (*and may very well do that one day*). As you think about your business, taking time to reflect and let go, this story and these guidelines inspire you to take a leap of faith or embrace the practical benefits of a Sabbath.

Or, you might just be curious about what would happen if you did it.

Removing The Safety Net Could Be Your Pathway To Success

In The Dark Knight Rise[5], Batman is broken and imprisoned by the villain (*Bane*). The prison is essentially a large hole in the ground with a view to the sky. Freedom is visible but impossible to access (*or so it seems*).

The prisoners can see the escape. There is a series of small platforms that go upward around the sizeable round tunnel and out of the prison, but the last two hard-to-access slabs contain a distance that's impossible to jump. Legend has it; someone did make that jump.

Along with these platforms is a safety rope. When someone attempting to jump towards the last platform slips, the rope prevents their fall (*and their brutal death*).

---

[5] *The Dark Knight Rises.* Dir. Christopher Nolan. Perf. Christian Bale. Warner Brothers, 2012.

After recovering from his injuries, Bruce Wayne (*Batman*) ties himself to the rope and attempts to escape unsuccessfully. The last platform (*for exiting the prison*) is just too far to jump and land successfully. Each time he jumps and falls, the rope catches him, preventing an untimely (*and anti-climactic*) death.

But, he's heard of the legend of someone escaping before.

How did they do it?

How did they get out of this prison?

How did they gain their freedom?

She jumped without the rope.

When success means either freedom or death, the jumper must give everything and hold nothing back. This mentality and this tension were required for Bruce Wayne to escape. If you've seen the film, you know he successfully lands on the platform after making the jump untethered (*with the risk of death*).

Completely unable to succeed in the jump with the safety of the rope, jumping without was the riskiest action he could take. His life was at stake.

Batman had a choice. Imprisonment or freedom with the chasm of risk in between.

You have that choice; to jump, for your business.

Will you choose to stay in your comfort and safety zone, or will you decide the freedom is worth the risk?

For me, the Sabbath year and eventual decision to end the company was me letting go of the rope and jumping without any guarantees. It could have all ended horrifically but instead was a catalyst for transforming my life, marriage, and vocational path.

Now, while my inspirational journey may provide you with ideas, it's likely to unfold differently than it has for me.

As you read through the remainder of the book, I'll guide you through the practical steps, underlying this process, you must take to prepare for the jump. I'll lead you to the edge, but it'll be up to you to take action.

Learning to let go, and recognizing your striving, as an indicator that something's off, will be your challenge to reconcile.

Maybe you're not fully committed to the business. When we are, and going in the right direction, striving is not something we struggle to overcome.

I came face-to-face with this question of commitment. If I were to start over vocationally, would I choose to launch and sustain a marketing company? Was I fully committed, or was I holding back?

Sounds like the perfect time to share the full story of Noodlehead Marketing.

5. The Noodlehead Marketing Story

Starting in 2007, I set out to create a company, a vehicle that'd take me towards my dreams & passions. Instead of arriving there, we arrived at a state of survival and isolation. I was leading the charge.

After going the wrong direction for some time, we stopped and altered our course, and set out to create a thriving company with a purpose, striving towards a unified vision.

After living our vision internally (*intentional companies reflecting excellence*), while externally helping other companies do the same, the transition unexpectedly led to the year of release (*Sabbath Year*) where I'd eventually let the company go.

Sharing our story provides you inspiration and an example to dive in, lean on the difficult, and ultimately move towards intentionality and sustainability.

It'll illuminate that it was challenging, and I floundered to lead and take courage. But, through the process, there was a series of powerful transformations towards a new and better future.

In the following section, we'll shift perspectives as we explore the seven-year Noodlehead Marketing story **authored by my wife, Caitlyn Montoya,** and told from the perspective of the business narrator.

How We Started

Long before Noodlehead Marketing Jason Scott Montoya had his curls, he was a fun-loving, energetic teenage boy. People loved him for his uncanny ability to weave together fun, and adventure where anyone could participate. The name *'Noodlehead'* stemmed from his fun-loving nature as he called anyone he thought was silly or goofy a Noodlehead. When he finally grew his hair out and discovered his natural curls, the name turned back on him, and though not the original Noodlehead, he became the most memorable.

Attracted to his fun-loving nature and his love of Jesus, Caitlyn, became a part of his makeshift short film production team. Their friendship blossomed into love and, in 2005, the two married. They moved from their hometown in Arizona to Atlanta in hopes of pursuing their dreams of telling stories through feature films.

The Years of Heartache

Many were hurt as we struggled to find our voice and identity. Some were run over by us as we rushed towards a goal, and others were left behind confused as we got distracted by the busyness that surrounded us.

After two years of being newlyweds full-time students, the pair succeeded in growing Noodlehead Studios (*Its first name*). Their focus shifted full-time into launching this company and generating revenue to support the films the couple hoped to create. Their goals and aspirations seemed noble enough on the surface; they wanted to weave CS Lewis style stories and spread the love of Jesus through the film medium.

However, they soon discovered, as many young entrepreneurs do, that unless you are highly focused and intentional, you can quickly become a slave to your dreams.

Noodlehead Studios was a full-service creative company offering a wide range of products and services. We successfully generated a living for the pair as well as a team of talented people.

Through all this *"success"* they became distracted from their original goal, to share the love of Jesus through thought-provoking stories. Their entire lives were a slave to the company in the early years, with the offices taking up all but one small room in the couples 1,100 square foot condo home.

Had this company been their dream, had they set out to create a creative service marketing company, perhaps the tight quarters wouldn't have taken such a toll on them. This business wasn't their dream though, Noodlehead Marketing was just a means to an end, and also a marital wedge.

As teens, Jason and Caitlyn had both valued friendships and relationships. Quality time spent with people getting to know them on a deeper level is at the core of who the pair is. The breakneck pace they kept, and the rapid unstructured growth they experienced, made for less than excellent communication and no accountability. This approach led to many failed relationships. In a visceral way, they hurt and were hurt by people they loved and cared for beyond the business they were doing with them. These hurts hardened many hearts.

A Call to Change

We sought out clarity and understanding and began to redeem some broken patterns and relationships from our past.

Shortly after the birth of their first child, and Caitlyn's exit from the company, Jason began to look at where they were and what they had become. He didn't like what he saw. He didn't like the direction the company was heading or the message it was portraying to the world. Jason didn't like the dynamics or the culture he had cultivated. Together with a great team at his side, he began working on changing Noodlehead Studios into Noodlehead Marketing.

Having always had friends that were practically family growing up, Jason wanted to create a culture of family, a workplace and environment from which the employees wanted to work. He desired a place where the staff of highly talented artists could come and feel safe to be creative. He wanted his team to know that relationships were more important than getting another dollar to fund a feature film.

The Noodlehead team came up with a code by which we would all operate. Structures and systems that allowed for creativity and individual voices to be a part of the everyday. Knowing that *intentional organizations reflect excellence*, our purpose shifted to being an example of excellence and accountability to inspire others. We committed to be *passionate*, to *love*, to *respect*, to *serve*, to *actively change to become better* and *always listen and share ideas*.

In 2012, we implemented our vision and were pushing forward in our mission. We had finally become a great company, the kind of company where us Noodleheads could proudly share. While it seemed great, there were still undercurrents of resentment floating through it all. Resentment between Jason and Caitlyn and the stress the company had put on their marriage, resentment between Jason and the company because it just wasn't his dream or his passion.

A Leap Of Faith

After operating with intentionality and being an excellent company, we thought redeeming our past errors was the end of the story, but this stage taught us, there was more. The communication flowed excellently, and employees and clients were held accountable leading to great work. We began to get a fuller picture of the reconciliation God had in store for us as a company.

Amid this heyday, we found ourselves homeless. We had to move out of the space we had been occupying and into a smaller transitional office. While we searched for a new home, we lost our largest client due to the change in our business model. It felt as though we were being ushered into another season of transition, so the team called for prayer and direction as to our next step.

After discussing the situation, Jason encouraged his wife to pray for guidance. The answers she gave them directed the team to a Levitical text concerning the Sabbath year (*Shemitah*), a year of rest and release. The team did a small Bible study on the text and set up guidelines and boundaries concerning the year. They then paused to think about it some more, and finally unanimously came to the agreement that the company would take a Sabbath year.

If things were going great, why would we decide to suddenly stop everything, change, and take a leap of faith?

After turning our wheels full speed for six years, we learned that God's timing is perfect. We could run the race full-speed, or we could walk it, but God's timing is perfect and can't be changed.

At first, we hoped it would only be a year of rest and release from the past resentments and hurts formed after years of operating poorly with no intentionality. Many of us hoped and expected that with the release from these past mistakes a new Noodlehead business would emerge, one more financially diversified able to launch into our next season with ease and comfort.

However, in the final months, it became apparent this company, while great, was not anyone's dream or vision for serving God. As much as Jason had changed the company, it could never remove the pain and hardships that it had caused his marriage early on.

The Noodlehead team will always be family, but it was time for the team to leave the nest. Taking what they learned, they launched into a more focused purpose and vision for the next phase of their lives.

Moving Forward

The decision to shut down did not mean we failed or that we no longer believed in the systems and processes we created. Quite the contrary, we believed in them very much. These tools we created were an integral part of the next stage of our journey, helping us integrate with new companies and teams. They were our parting gift to our family, our followers, our clients, and now you.

In all that you do, be intentional. Following this model equips us and our projects to be great. They help us weed through the distractions that come along.

It is a process Caitlyn and Jason wish they had when they started Noodlehead Studios.

This process would have saved them many follies and distractions along the road. And they are the many pieces of the puzzle you have read so far in this book and will continue to glean from the remaining chapters.

Part Two: Moving Forward

6. Step One - Transform Your Business By Leveling Yourself Up
7. Step Two - Build A Strong Business Foundation
8. Step Three - Lead Your Dedicated Team Forward
9. Step Four - Elevate Your Business With Bullet-Proof Systems & Mental Models
10. A Five-Phase Process For Transforming Your Messy Business Into A Well Oiled Machine
11. My Parting Words To The Visionary Business Owner
12. Standing On The Edge

6. Step One - Transform Your Business By Leveling Yourself Up

The Peter principle states, *"We rise to the level of our respective incompetence."* As entrepreneurs, we grow the business as far as we're able to push it, but at some point, we lack the maturity, capacity, and ability to move it to the desired state (*which we've likely not defined*).

New business owners struggle to shift their chaotic business. However, the limit is not outside of us (*knowledge or skills*), it's inside (*character and maturity*). We won't ever take our team to success if we don't level up.

As effective leaders, we're required to face circumstances, act when we don't feel like it, proactively solve problems that seem to spring up at the worst times, evolve with the trends and marketplace, rest and rejuvenate along the way, and lead those who follow us when we don't have much left to give. Yes, it's complex.

Just reading that might make you feel overwhelmed. Living it is an entirely different scenario. But, the type of leader required to inspire your team to the desired destination, is just out of your reach.

You're not quite whom you need to be to get there, your team is not mature enough to catalyze you there, and your circumstances are not challenging enough to force a change.

Often, we seek to hire someone else that will fix everything, only to be perpetually disappointed when they don't (*because we've unrealistically expected too much*).

So how do we begin the transformation? How do we become a new and better leader? We do it by starting with a growth trajectory snapshot.

Knowing the path we're on, and where it leads will provide the essential ingredients for accelerating the transformation process. While it won't be easy, the fruit far outweighs the cost.

Thus, **you enter the heart of the book.** To transform will require you to traverse the following five areas to turn into the leader necessary to move your organization to sustainability.

I. Understanding Your Growth Trajectory, & How You Accelerate The Journey
II. Internal Dive: Facing Your Fears & Knowing Yourself

III. Embracing Reality & Accepting Responsibility
IV. Leading Courageously & Operating Wisely
V. Outwardly Manifesting Your Transformation

Let's begin with the foundation and understanding of how this growth journey will unfold.

I. Understanding Your Growth Trajectory, & How You Accelerate The Journey

> "...the self-authored form of mind does not want to be written by our circumstances; we figure instead out how to pick up the pen to write our own story." - Jennifer Garvey Berger, Unlocking Leadership Mindtraps

There's a past or future moment in our lives when we face the truth of how unequipped we are to handle life (*and our business*). What we were taught or told growing up doesn't match up to what we experience. And, it fails to prepare us for the challenges we encounter in relationships, work, and community.

At this point, we either shift the blame to others or look in the mirror and take responsibility, to self-author who we'll be going forward, and how we'll interact with the world around us.

For many, this becomes a midlife crisis where they choose to point the finger elsewhere, acting detrimental to self and others.

The rest choose to embrace the challenges and take responsibility for what they can control, which is ultimately how they live their life and respond to the circumstances (*even unfair ones*) that come their way.

The Adult Development Process

This moment of crisis is an opportunity for us to shift from level three to level four in the well-researched adult developmental theory (*Constructive Developmental Framework*).

This psychological explanation courses human maturity over five leadership levels (*or lenses*) as described *by Keith Eigel and Karl Kuhnert (The Map), and Robert Kegan (In Over Our Heads*), for how we see and experience the world.

With extensive research behind it, Constructive Developmental Theory[6] informs the potential we have to traverse five stages of development. Knowing these stages helps us understand where we are, where we're going, and how to move along the path.

---

[6]To explore Constructive Developmental Theory further, check out The Map: Your Path To Effectiveness In Leadership, Life, & Legacy by Keith M. Eigel, PhD & Karl W. Kuhnert, PhD.

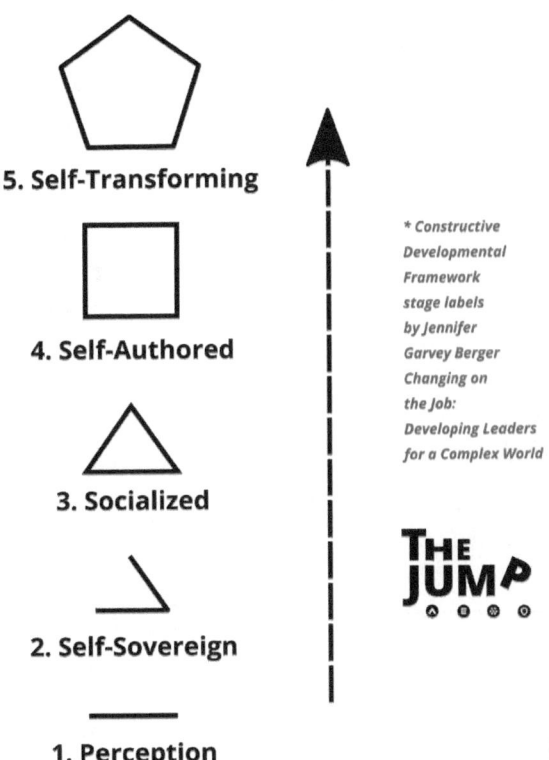

The first three stages are categorized as an externally shaped level of maturity. For the first several years of our lives, we're molded by how we perceive the world around us. A Nickel is larger than a Dime; therefore, it must be worth more.

In our early teenage years, we begin to understand the rules of the world we live in, at least in a simplistic form and within proximity. Our emotional health is heavily influenced by whether we're winning or losing, and it's highly challenging to know or communicate more

---

[7] Berger, Jennifer Garvey. *Changing on the Job: Developing Leaders for a Complex World*. Stanford University Press. 2013.

complex and nuanced layers of truth in this second stage (*Self-Sovereign*).

In the third stage (*Socialized*), we recognize other people as partners in accomplishing our individual goals. Empathy enters in, and we see needs outside ourselves. New influences, especially ones we choose (*or think we've chosen*), take a more significant stake in influencing us. Peer pressure and approval drive (*or constrain*) our behavior, sometimes more than we'd like.

Like the first two stages, our incomplete perspective of the world will face irreconcilable differences giving birth to the fourth stage (*Self-Authored*) of self-composition (*once we take responsibility*).

We've decided for ourselves who we are, and the underlying facets that determine our identity and core beliefs. While we often retain the perspectives of earlier levels, they hold less weight on how we see ourselves and the world. And, over time, our crafted paradigm will lead to effectively accomplishing and harmonizing our goals personally and professionally.

As I mentioned earlier, some point along the way, we'll face more profound and complex challenges we won't be able to smash through with our effective way of doing things. It's at this final transition where we must let go our of our paradigm, just long enough to open up to other possibilities involving core values, and the harmonization of multiple entities and agendas. Consider Martin Luther King Jr. & Abraham Lincoln in their latter years as level five (*Self-Transforming*) leader examples.

While I encourage you to explore the adult growth model, my focus in this book is addressing the transition as a business owner from level three onward.

As a level three leader, the business is you and vice versa. When it's doing well, you're doing well. And when it's not, you're going to feel it. The business roller coaster dictates your personal state, and often reflects it. My business name was Noodlehead Marketing, and it was derived from my personal nickname. In retrospect, it's clear how much my identity was grafted with the company.

As a level four leader, we are a person with a business. It's something separate we do but is distinctly independent. We and others influence the company. This separation helps us better understand and lead the company in an objective way.

On average, we humans tend to become level three dominant in our early twenties, and in our mid-forties, we're locked in at level four. Level five is found in or beyond our sixties (*on average*).

But, transitioning from childhood to adulthood is not easy. We all go through the experience, and we all travel it in varying ways, with different perspectives under unique but similar circumstances. So, how does one move through these stages of maturity?

Vertical Development.

As opposed to lateral development, which is the accumulation of knowledge, vertical growth (*"Insight that changed you." Karl W. Kuhnert, Ph.D., The Map*) is how you know what you know, and why you believe what you do. It's a deep-rooted insight that shapes behavior and elevates maturity.

> "Vertical development would entail understanding the purpose or value of conflict in a new, different, and increasingly more complete way... Challenging life experiences either accelerate or arrest vertical growth. The more challenging the experience, the greater its potential to bring about vertical development." - Keith Eigel, Ph.D., Co-author of The Map: Your Path to Effectiveness in Leadership, Life, and Legacy

It's these challenges we face that create the perfect soup for meaningful and profound growth. But, we must embrace them to receive the gift.

> "Once the storm is over, you won't remember how you made it through, how you managed to survive. You won't even be sure, whether the storm is really over. But one thing is certain. When you come out of the storm, you won't be the same person who walked in. That's what this storm's all about." - Haruki Murakami

For entrepreneurs, we'll face what feels like perpetual storms. It seems as one ends, the next is right around the corner.

While the emotional weight of these challenges may seem unbearable, it's this very tension that fuels the fire for us to become the very leader we need to be and to lead the company we want to create.

So, for us to move our company out of the cycle of mediocrity requires we look in the mirror to discover the person looking back at us. For us to transform our business, we must become greater today than we were yesterday.

And, It starts with facing your fears (*by knowing yourself*), continues with embracing reality (*and accepting responsibility*), wisely operating (*how we do it matters*), and choosing how we'll interact with others (*people matter most*).

> "Don't wait for extraordinary opportunities. Seize common occasions and make them great. Weak men wait for opportunities; great men make them."
> — Orison Swett Marden

But, these don't just happen on their own. These efforts require intentionality, the core trait of stage four. And facing fears won't happen without it.

To tackle this challenge, there's no better person to help us navigate facing our fears than Rocky Balboa.

II. Internal Dive: Facing Your Fears & Knowing Yourself

> "All of humanity's problems stem from man's inability to sit quietly in a room alone." - Blaise Pascal

From 2009-2010, I went through a year of floundering and exploration as I sought to ground my identity and purpose. A few years after moving across the country, launching a business, and being married, my life and business unraveled into a roller coaster of horror and excitement. There were great times, and there were rock bottom moments. As ambitious and bold as I was, I was not prepared for life's beating.

In Rocky Balboa (# 6), the movie, there's a personal and powerful sequence where the Italian Stallion shares with his son how he used to hold him and wonder about his future. He goes on to say the following, which at the time, felt like he was speaking to me.

> *"Then the time came for you to be your own man and take on the world, and you did. But somewhere along the line, you changed. You stopped being you. You let people stick a finger in your face and tell you you're no good. And when things got hard, you started looking for something to blame, like a big shadow.*
>
> *Let me tell you something you already know. The world ain't all sunshine and rainbows. It's a very mean and nasty place, and I don't care how tough you are it will beat you to your knees and keep you there permanently if you let it. You, me, or nobody is gonna hit as hard as life." - Rocky Balboa*

Entrepreneurs know and viscerally feel this. As pioneers in our lives, we're forced to face issues and lead people who look up to us. Excited by the prospect on the onset, we're nowhere near prepared to make it happen. And many don't.

But for those fully committed and the leaders who want to get up and move forward, they have another choice. Rocky Balboa's monologue continues.

> *"But it ain't about how hard you hit. It's about how hard you can get hit and keep moving forward.* ***How much you can take and keep moving forward.*** *That's how winning is done!*
>
> *Now if you know what you're worth, then go out and get what you're worth. But ya gotta be willing to take the hits, and not pointing fingers saying you ain't where you wanna be because of him, or her, or anybody!*
>
> *Cowards do that and that ain't you! You're better than that!"* - Rocky Balboa

How about you? Are you ready to lay the blame aside, look in the mirror, take the hits and move forward no matter how hard the upward climb?

At my most difficult point, I decided to move forward, to anchor into my purpose, and while it eventually got better, the transition was brutal. At multiple times along the way, I felt like giving up. You might have heard the following words, *'give up because you have already lost.'*

It could come from someone else but likely will be a voice inside your head. The tormenting fear as you strive to lead others and do something great. Along the way, we mess up and fail, and these failures have consequences (*emotionally & physically*).

A few years after moving to Atlanta, Georgia, life got hard. My wife and I moved across the country as newlyweds trying to survive (*quite the opposite of my flourishing upbringing*). Life, work, relationships, and faith spiraled into chaos.

As I looked down the road of my impending fate, I made a decision. Running life my way was not working, and I needed help.

When you get to the point where you hear a message from fear, you'll have a choice. You can succumb to this fear and give in. Alternatively, you can face your fears head-on. And the truth is, this step may be the first of many that lead to carrying an even heavier and harder burden (*but much more meaningful*).

For me, this involved prayer for divine guidance (*God, my way is not working, show me yours!*) and learning from the people around me, even when we don't want to or when they don't helpfully communicate feedback.

When pride rises and fear rules, will you let go of them both? Will you persevere when failure is before you? Will you do what is right when life is pressing down on you?

For me, it was impossible on my own. I needed God's direction and the support of the community around me.

And over time with His healing, I looked in the mirror, faced my fears, swallowed my pride, and took responsibility. They were none of the things I wanted to do, but all the actions essential to moving my faith, life, family, and community forward.

And it's the step I believe you too can make. It's the one you must take when you hear the words, '*give up. you've already lost.*'

Once you're ready to own that the perpetual roller coaster you've been on is due in large part to your decisions, you're prepared to look into that mirror and see what reflects back at you.

III. Embracing Reality & Accepting Responsibility

It's almost impossible to launch a small business without taking at least some responsibility for yourself and the business. The question is, have you taken full responsibility while also understanding the full reality of what you're facing, and what's involved in running a company?

It's not easy. After we embrace our decision-making ability (*agency*), we're likely to flop and flounder.

Eventually, we get to a place where we understand these challenges and invite them into the fold for further sharpening. In this state, an invited plan helps us move forward in a meaningful and sustained way.

But as mentioned earlier, we won't get to this glorious destination until we lead courageously and take responsibility.

Responsibility Swapping

In multiple seasons of life, I've waited (*many times subconsciously*) for someone else to take the burden of responsibility from me and do what's necessary. When work is hard, it's easy to fall into this trap.

In the Island Story[8], I call this the Visionary Stage and a jaded visionary is the Turtle (*a distraction*). The Turtle wants others to carry them, and ironically enough, they also carry other people's burdens, especially ones where the other person should be carrying it themselves.

Inappropriate responsibility swapping gives people significance, but also fosters toxic dynamics.

What they expect and what they do are crisscrossed in different aspects of their lives. It'd be like a parent who should direct their kids to clean up after themselves, but instead does it for them. But they expect their spouse to clean up after them when they should do it for themselves.

Visionaries are going so hard, so fast, in so many directions they tangle everything up. When they stay in this tangled state, they get stuck and become jaded towards others.

Visionaries In The Workplace

The same dynamic plays out with people in the workplace. Business owners earn more money and hire more people. They believe that hiring more people will solve their problems and alleviate the burden. However, when they hire in this chaotic state of poor self-management, the situation only gets more challenging.

---

[8] You can read the Island Story in its entirety at www.WhatIsTheIslandStory.com

If you're struggling because you must do more than is sustainable, and you start hiring people, there is a high likelihood these people are only going to make your burden heavier and lead to more significant issues. And your many visions will be left on the business battlefield as broken promises.

Waiting For Rescue, While Abstaining From Responsibility

In 2010, after difficult years in the business, I was waiting for the company to be successful. I was waiting for the right person to come along and fulfill my vision for the company. He or she was to take us to the "*promised land*" only to end up perpetually disappointed when it never happened.

And that's the key. While others can aid us along the way, they cannot carry our burdens to the final destination.

Not Doing Hard Things While Waiting For Rescue Leads To Death

In October 2010, I first met my friend Joe Kissack, author of the Fourth Fisherman. If you're unfamiliar with the story, years ago five Mexican fishermen were stranded at sea for nine months, and three survived. They had nothing except a Bible, their faith, and each other. Joe integrated, into the book, his challenging life story with the fishermen's fantastic journey of survival.

Upon learning the premise on a chance encounter with the author, I immediately wanted to know why three survived and the other two died.

It turns out; their death was the result of "waiting" for rescue, and an unwillingness to do the hard work required for survival. Waiting for rescue at sea for almost a year without doing anything eliminates all chances of survival, obviously. We operate this way all the time.

In a terrible situation, like being lost at sea, it is easy to feel hopeless and helpless because so many elements are out of our control. But, there were still essential actions the fishermen could do, like taming their mind, catching food, collecting rainwater, reading their Bible, and talking to each other.

What became apparent to me in learning this was how I'd been "*waiting*" for rescue in my business. I was waiting for certain aspects of the company to take themselves to my desired location. When I was not waiting, I was daydreaming about future goals based on when circumstances would allow them instead of taking actions to move towards them today. I was letting life happen to me instead of leading how God intended. My true self was further reflected back, and I didn't like what I saw.

A Desire To Avoid Hard Work & The Test Of Our Character

When we're face-to-face with the clarity that hard work is necessary to move forward and make progress, we can subconsciously hope a distraction finds us.

"Please, let anything come up, so I don't have to do the hard task in front of me," we think.

And when we're avoiding responsibility, we love this type of distraction. We hope someone or something that will do the hard work for us. Oswald Chambers says it well.

> "Drudgery is one of the finest tests to determine the genuineness of our character. Drudgery is work that is far removed from anything we think of as ideal work. It is the utterly hard, menial, tiresome, and dirty work. And when we experience it, our spirituality is instantly tested, and we will know whether or not we are spiritually genuine." - Oswald Chambers, My Utmost For His Highest

Ouch.

A Little Help To Push Me Along

In 2010, I sought out a tool to help me navigate this weakness. Follow through was a constant challenge for me. While I was great in my interactions with people, give it time, and I'd fall off the wagon. With a growing business, I left many unsold deals on the table simply because they faded into the background.

This upfront zeal followed by silence impacted my relationship with God, my marriage, and my business. I was reactive, never consistently proactive.

My Adaptability and compelling charisma allowed me to repair and reconcile what I broke along the way, but over time, it stopped working. The cynicism of those around me set in.

Charm was no longer going to get me out of the holes I dug. So, I was forced to find a way to live consistently, but it meant facing two prominent problems.

The first was prioritizing the writing down of what needed to get done. Second, was being accountable to these documented activities. I created a spreadsheet with seven things I needed to do each week, with several actions to be done daily. No matter how crazy every week got, what were the weekly clockwork activities that would move this business forward?

This intentional focus would help set the stage for carrying forward the momentum.

A Passionate Short Term Run

Like usual, I had another great run of four weeks, but it quickly went down to zero. I lacked the discipline and habits to live out of the system. And, my friends dropped the ball in holding me accountable. Without self-accountability and others checking in on me, it was destined to fail. So, it did.

So for a while, I fell off the wagon. Inconsistency continued to be my biggest problem. I kept trying to use different tools, programs, and devices to '*fix me*,' but I was never able to cure the bug of my weaknesses.

Preparing For A Marathon, Step By Step

I attended a conference where Jim Collins spoke about his book, Great by Choice, and his study of successful leaders versus unsuccessful ones. During his talk, he made the following comment "**mediocrity is the sign of chronic inconsistency!**". That statement hit me right in the forehead like a two-by-four, and it was the inspiration I needed to change.

I finally recognized my need to start small and work my way up. I focused on an action, mastered it, and then added more. The idea was to master one thing regularly and then add to it. I had been too focused on growing the business and then mastering.

While chaotically attempting to run a marathon without any training led to an abundance of failure, a few months of habit management practice allowed me to catch my breath and consistently succeed at my weekly goals.

The result? In Q1 of 2012, our company revenue grew twenty-five percent compared to the previous year. After several months of consistent activity, the impact was felt and real. This real-life and owned experience anchored this lesson inside me.

The habit management tool[9] became my activity correction device, a *'behavioral chiropractor,'* and it eventually corrected my *"action."* If I wanted to modify an existing behavior or habit, develop a new action or stop one, I used my tool to make it happen. This underlying commitment drove it ongoing.

So finally, after numerous failed attempts and multiple distractions, I was gaining traction. And it also quickly became apparent how often I was busy, but not productive (*towards the end game*).

Slow & Steady Wins The Race

The story of the tortoise and the hare is a good metaphor for this dynamic. The hare runs ahead and almost finishes the race, but falls asleep only to wake up behind and doing everything it can to catch up and win.

Unfortunately, it's too late. The slow and steady well-paced and sustainable tortoise wins. While running the race as a hare has benefits, it won't last for the long run. When we watch enough tortoises pass us by, we start to realize the problem with our approach.

Adversity, we come to find, acts as a powerful motivator for moving us forward.

---

[9] Visit www.jasonscotttmontoya.com/jump to download the toolbox that helps me succeed as a small business owner.

The Uninvited Challenges Help Us Grow

As much as we might resist the idea, hard times could save your life, or empower you to have an amazing one.

In 2010, a documentary film came out called Catfish[10]. The movie documents a guy, Nev, meeting and falling in love with a girl, Megan, whom he met on the Internet. After numerous canceled attempts to meet up with this girl from another state, Nev spontaneously decides to see her in-person.

Unfortunately, his out-of-state arrival illuminates a tragic situation with Megan and her family. Nothing is as it seemed, and the entire relationship was a fraud.

At the end of the movie, a family member shares the story of where the film gets its name.

> "They used to take cod from Alaska all the way to China and keep them in ship vats. By the time the vats reached China, the flesh was mushy and tasteless. So this guy came up with the idea that if you put these cod in big vats, put some catfish in with them, the catfish will keep the Cod agile (as the catfish nip at them).
>
> There are those people who are catfish in life, and they keep you on your toes. They keep you guessing, they keep you thinking, they keep you fresh. And, I thank God for the catfish because we'd be droll,

---

[10] *Catfish.* Dir. Henry Joost and Ariel Schulman. Perf. Nev Schulman. Universal Pictures, 2010.

boring, and dull if we didn't have someone nipping at our fin." - Vince Wesselman, Catfish

Thanks to the way the universe is, we've got numerous natural catfish to keep us agile. For example, we need to provide for our needs, things decay, and other people with their competing agendas surround us. There is an abundance of catfish around to keep us moving forward and helping us develop character. We invite some catfish while others are ones we'd prefer to go away.

Unfortunately, success paired with complacency has a way of shielding us from these natural catfish. With the heavy burden that comes with providing for my family, having student loan debt and other family responsibilities, I get tired of these catfish nipping at me. *"Let me out of the tank so I can take a break!"* I think to myself. But, there is an inherent value.

Appreciating The Benefit Of These Challenges

While we all want relief from the unwanted tension of our reality, we must ensure our relief is only short-lived. Let's take time for rest and release, but let's make sure we don't eliminate every catfish in our life.

Now that our student loans are paid off, and the kids are maturing, the question bouncing in my head is, *'Will I drift backward without this organic tension?'*

The key for successful people not becoming delusional is to continue simulating catfish in their life when it's not required. This insight comes from someone comfortable amid success only to find my neglect of business and relationships, leading to severe problems. While the difficulty of our work can feel frustrating when we're not making progress, it also acts as a powerful and positive force keeping us on the right track and preventing us from causing harm (*to self or others*).

There is a story in the Hebrew Bible about a man named Job. Job goes from prosperity to losing everything and facing immense suffering. Three of his friends go back and forth about why this is happening, and his friends blame his suffering on some sin he committed. Eventually, a young observer (*Elihu*) steps into the conversation and shares the following message exposing Job's lack of perspective and Job's friend's ignorance.

> *"Suffering may be decreed for the righteous as a protection against greater sin, for moral betterment and warning, and to elicit greater trust and dependence on a merciful, compassionate God amid adversity." - Elihu.*[11]

While we can bring upon ourselves suffering and adversity, it can also act as a gift (*if we embrace it*). As Elihu shares his message, he's summarizing the catfish mechanism.

It's one we easily struggle to find value in because it feels like someone has robbed us and that we don't deserve what comes our way. It takes experience and

---

[11] "Elihu (Job)." Wikipedia.org, 17 September 2017, https://en.wikipedia.org/wiki/Elihu_(Job). Accessed July 7th 2018.

perspective to embrace the catfish concept. But once we do, our lives are changed for the better.

An Uninvited Catfish In My Life

Shortly after I shut down the company, I was emotionally hit with what felt like an oncoming train. Overwhelmed with emotion, I faced panic attacks and a roller coaster of anxiety and depression.

It lasted prominently for three months, but eventually, with the support of God and my community (*including some key insights from my dad*), I got up and moved forward. As I walked upwards and against the metaphorical river flow, my strength and focus increased. I was much better as a result of this trial by fire that very well could have consumed and destroyed me (*and for many, it does*).

While this roller coaster of anxiety and subsequent depression is no longer as strong or dominant in my life as it once was, there are still moments and days where these mental and emotional forces are strong. They're a helpful reminder of my limitations and need. It's an unpleasant but invited humility check to recognize how dependent I am on God and community. We can't do life alone.

This force also helps me recognize my limitations and desire to take on more than I can realistically handle. With my personality, I've historically lived an overcommitted life doing more than I want or should. But, these experiences are part of the reason I'm now more deliberate and iterative in my commitments.

In addition to my anxiety catfish, I also experience challenges living and guiding my chaotic family, working with stress-inducing company founders, getting sick, forgetting about a scheduled meeting, or dying in my habit management system to name five examples.

My mindset is geared to look at and lean into this tension as a way to grow myself, help others, and move us all forward towards a shared vision. My vision for you is to embrace these catfish and learn how to leverage them for positive outcomes.

Are You Finally Sick Of The Up & Down Cycle?

It's not until we realize there is no path or answer to hard menial work other than to do it, that we begin to change.

Embrace what feels like an unpleasant reality (*but ends up being a meaningful one*).

After an extended season, I was finally tired of this rat race hamster wheel. I wanted to make progress, not just go in circles.

So I buckled down, surveyed the horizon, and decided on what were the most important things I need to accomplish every week. These were my twenty-mile marches[12] (*the things that we must do consistently*). I established a community to encourage me forward, and it began with a singular focus.

---

[12] Collins, James: Great by Choice. HarperBusiness, 2011.

In a season of personal crisis, a friend once told me, your life can really only be about one or two things, so decide this focus ahead of time.

Initially, I sought a superficial answer to my problems, a silver bullet, but what I really needed was a life foundation change. I had to anchor my life on a rock, and only then did I realize how powerful discipline could be for me.

A Shift To Proactivity

> *"A ready person never needs to get ready -- He is ready."* - Oswald Chambers

These preceding revelations helped me focus on preparing for my future. Waiting, like the dead fishermen, would only perpetuate the current context and would eliminate my ability to respond when the opportunities rose up.

Oswald Chambers anchors this lesson deeply.

> *"When it comes to taking the initiative against drudgery (hard, menial or dull work), we have to take the first step as though there were no God. There is no point in waiting for God to help us— He will not. But once we arise, immediately we find He is there...If we will arise and shine, drudgery will be divinely transformed."*

After meeting Joe (*author of the Fourth Fisherman*) and embracing this revelation, I stepped up and did what I needed to do until finally, it paid off and we had a breakthrough.

As the leader of Noodlehead Marketing, I anchored into a self-authored and tested identity. Paired with a set vision for the company, 2011 became the year where we followed through on whom we said we were and the commitments we made. When we couldn't, we held ourselves accountable. 2011 was known to us Noodleheads as the year of intentionality.

If you find yourself in a place of waiting, buckle down and see what you can do to make your life and work better today.

When we act on these steps and push through to the other side where we consistently move, even when we don't feel like it, you'll find it's deeply satisfying (*like sharks constantly moving to keep oxygen flowing over their gills*).

But, we can't truly take these steps until we've taken ownership and responsibility for our lives, and our success. We must stop expecting this progress without the hard work consistently done over time.

Instead, embrace it.

Real success won't happen until you do.

A Five-Pronged Strategy For Leading Yourself (& *Eventually Your Business*) Forward

For those looking to accept the truth, and take responsibility, there are five simple but powerful ways you can move forward in your life. Each provides a different benefit, but as a collective action list diversifies our reliance (*should one fail, the others help shore up the dropped tension*).

- **Document Your Focus & Commit To Your Twenty-mile March (*what must happen weekly?*):** What do you want to accomplish in your business? What is the one primary action done consistently over time that will move you towards this destination? Identify this focus metric and commit. No matter what comes up, you make sure it gets done. Hold on, like a dog to a bone.
- **Personal Accountability With a Habit Management Tool:** With your focus metric, and secondary activities known, place them into a tracking tool, so you know what they are, and how you've fared at completing them. Results vary, but one thing is for sure, a habit management tool will surface many insights about yourself and circumstances and will give visibility to the very daily activities you must do.
- **Peer Accountability Through a Small Group or Contrasting Friendship:** While it's uplifting to surround ourselves with people who encourage and celebrate with us, we also need to surround ourselves with people willing to challenge and ask us questions, even when we resist. Groups and strong friendships contribute to this level of accountability.
- **Elder Accountability in a Coach or Mentor:** There's always someone further up the metaphorical life stairs who could shed valuable insight and perspective to help us grow. Ideally,

we're in a relationship with a well-grounded and value-centric leader who pushes us further and higher than we'd ever do for ourselves.
- **Sharing Our Wisdom With Others:** As we journey up the stairs of life, there are those who are behind us, as well. As we progress, we help others succeed as others helped us. And, there's a hidden benefit about teaching, it helps us better understand and anchor what we know.

To embrace Catfish Living entirely, get focused, hold yourself accountable, be in dialogue with peers, submit yourself to guiding authority, and give insights to those following your footsteps.

Each of these relational dynamics provides us with different pieces of the perspective pie. Doing all five will ensure we have a complete picture to learn, grow, and lead.

IV. Lead Courageously & Operate Wisely

You've faced your fears, embraced responsibility, how will you respond?

After moderating a panel on how to navigate technology as a father, one of the guys from the group came up to me afterward. He was an older guy working in the technology field and felt as if he was getting left behind at work, something striving business owners feel as well.

The new guys were energetic and skilled, and it seemed their ability to adapt was far beyond his. His concern left him thinking; it was only a matter of time before his career would end.

As most of us know, technology tends to change so quickly; it can be difficult keeping up.

I remember in our marketing agency, this was a similar tension we faced. We offered a portfolio of digital marketing services in areas which were constantly changing. When we started, Myspace was still an important facet of a digital marketing campaign. Over the seven years in business, the space changed, and we always seemed to be falling behind the innovation curve.

The beauty of getting left behind is how it taught us to respond in these situations, and we learned about the reliable underlying bedrock available.

The first is knowing and anchoring into what we value most.

Priorities: What Matters Most?

> *"The difference between successful people and really successful people is that really successful people say no to almost everything." - Warren Buffett*

There is always something new, and there are always pioneers to explore it. The more I wasn't pioneering, the more I learned I didn't need to always innovate.

As an entrepreneur, pioneering was a part of my identity, but after the brutality of the role, I begin to rethink it. Pioneers tend to get beat up by the process of always being on the front lines, and when they persist at it too often for too long, it burns them out.

It is acceptable for us to stay back and be willing to learn from the pioneers when we are not able to be one. We don't have to explore every new thing. We can rest assured that time will filter out what is new, good, and not worthwhile. When Google Wave launched, I never joined, and eventually, it was shut down (*I did join Google Plus and it was shut down too*). While there is value in being the first to take advantage of a trending opportunity, sometimes it leads to our vision blur and ultimate failure.

When we have a choice between the seemingly infinite options of exploration, let's choose the singular option which helps us accomplish our objectives most effectively. It will require we say no to most ideas so we can say **YES!** to what matters most.

Time is limited; let's respond accordingly.

Build Relationships; They Matter More

> *"Clients do not come first. Employees come first. If you take care of your employees, they will take care of the clients."* - Richard Branson

The one thing worse than falling behind in technology and trends is falling behind in relationships.

Looking back, we at Noodlehead Marketing spent too much time chasing technology, and our chase resulted in many neglected team members and client relationships. Ideally, we want to maintain both, but when it comes to priorities, I believe the relationship is far more critical.

Take care of the team, and they'll take care of the clients. Moreover, clients will be more forgiving when we don't know about the latest widget and tool.

Also, while we may feel like we are falling behind in our area of work, the reality is that our client is likely much further behind us. To them, we are the pioneer (*even when we're not the industry pioneer*).

With my marketing business, we worked primarily in the home service industry (*Construction, Real Estate, etc.*), and our clients were a decade behind the mainstream marketing trends.

While companies focused on the latest, our clients attempted to understand what a website was and how it helped them. They didn't take building a website seriously until 2009! And, they had a highly successful business model without it. We met them where they were and spent the time to teach and bring them along.

On the flip-side, we might experience team members (*likely younger*) who are technologically way ahead of us. It is in these opportunities we can humble ourselves and ask them to teach us. By building strong team relationships, others can help carry the burden when we can't bear it ourselves. It's best when our entire team knows and does more than us.

Whether we are ahead or behind, building strong relationships equips us to face these challenges, and tap into something exponentially more long-lasting.

> "It doesn't make sense to hire smart people and then tell them what to do , We hire smart people so they can tell us what to do." - Steve Jobs

Be An Expert In Filling The Gap

In business, there are always gaps that need filling and opportunities that need tapping. Usually, the holes remaining, are the more complex, more laborious, or neglected.

When we look around our business, we see what works, what we or others have broken, and what's missing.

For many, they choose to see and not act, but it is those who see these gaps and decide to act who are most valuable. These types of experts are always desired and rare to find. It's how I've built and grown a successful consulting business.

A business that proactively searches for and fills gaps (*embracing opportunities and solving problems*) is far more valuable than the most naturally talented person in the company.

Finding and filling gaps requires a willingness to go above and beyond our call of duty, and it requires more work of us. Opportunities are in front of us; let's choose to be the leader who finds these gaps and fills them.

Explicit Communication

In conversation with a fellow freelancer, we discussed the general lack of responsiveness of people when we email, text, or call. Many times we send messages and don't hear back for days, even weeks. Sometimes we don't receive any feedback until we follow up numerous times. This lack of responsiveness happens with active clients and people with whom I have a relationship. When it comes to sales activities, the perpetrators are even worse.

I once landed a referred client because their freelancer went dark on the communication front. They had not heard from him in over thirty days, and they needed reliable help quickly. After working with them a few months, this freelancer reached back out seeking to start back up where they left off. As you can imagine, the client did not respond well.

I used to be the person who failed to respond. I struggled to maintain Inbox zero and reply to people in a reasonable amount of time (*including clients*). If you were not in my bubble (*literally*), it was going to be difficult to get updates.

I was overcommitted and did not have the discipline or capacity to manage my communications. There were times my lack of communication was so bad, I lost potential customers because, by the time I discovered their inquiry, they had already moved forward with another company.

There were several times I hired an assistant to help me process my messages, but they only exaggerated (*not alleviated*) the lack of structure and problems.

Now, I'm the opposite.

I over-communicate and respond quickly. If I can't give a meaningful answer, I'll at least note my receipt and let the other person know I'll respond later with a detailed response. I'm constantly giving clients updates weekly, and as I work on their project. I want my customers slightly annoyed at how often and thoroughly I communicate with them. I want to answer their questions before they ask.

The beauty of operating this way is it sets me apart from other freelancers and companies that offer what I do. Clients have a reliable partner that helps them grow their business, and they don't have to chase me down (*In fact, it's usually the opposite*). When I do have something unexpected or problematic arise, it's not a big deal because I've built so much relational and communication equity (*by prioritizing time pouring into the person*) that they know there is a good reason I'm not responding. It also provides them a trigger to reach out again or in another form if it's urgent.

This type of explicit communication is powerful, and doing it well will set you apart from everyone else.

Think Bigger And Become An Authority

When we felt like we were falling behind in our business, we began to shift towards a strategic mindset in our offerings. Regardless of how technology has changed, we always knew this strategy skill would be valuable.

Reading the ancient book, the Art of War, we learn about strategies of war. These same strategies of war are applicable today. Many of the principles (*symbolism, scale, communication, etc.*) apply to business. When we can implement strategies almost two thousand years later, it indicates that strategic work contains longevity.

So, we spent time and resources to become an expert in strategy. We intended to become an authority, and while challenging, it was rewarding.

As you experience seasons of falling behind, decide to think bigger and see the battlefield from a strategic angle. It'll also make it easier to resist the distractions.

Understanding The Four Types Of Distractions, We Face

When the iPad first came out, I'd play Zombie Highway. The point of the game is to drive as far as possible without dying (*by crashing*). The game seems easy, but forces are pushing back to escalate the difficulty. The car could crash either by running into debris in the road or it could flip over when there were too many zombies on the vehicle.

To succeed in the game required looking forward onto the horizon instead of at the zombies. Their presence was distracting and caused the player to focus on the horde instead of the road. In most cases, the zombies didn't flip the car, but focusing on them led to distracted driving, causing the player to crash into debris they didn't see coming. The loss of vision and visibility inevitably leads to a tragic ending.

There will be numerous zombies on your company (*vehicle*), and the overwhelming distractors will require you to stay focused on what matters (*the vision*), while adequately delegating our resources to handle the zombies. When you must deal with them directly, it's crucial to recognize you can't spend all your time resolving every single problem yourself; else you fall victim to unexpectedly crashing and burning your business.

Principally, there are four main distractions (*via the Island Story Framework*[13]) we come across. And falling prey to them is connected to what we need, or what is inherently motivating us.

- **Sharks prevent us from thinking.** They keep us distracted with what is absolute and push us away from uncertainty (*from a motivation of self-preservation*). Out of fear, we fail to explore

---

[13] The Island Story by Jason Scott Montoya can be read in it's entirely on whatistheislandstory.com

new ideas that could help us productively move forward or operate smarter. Launching a new business, or product could lead to our downfall (*we fear*)! Ironically, the sharks are continually recruiting us to help them survive, while we struggle to do so ourselves.

- **Clownfish prevent us from starting.** They keep us focused on mentally exploring the new and exciting ideas (*from a motivation for fun*), but they never let us act on them. As we're about to move forward with something, the clownfish shows us a new shiny idea, and we allow the previous thing to fade away. It's so hard to say no to fun things, so we never start anything.
- **Turtles prevent us from finishing.** They distract us with new causes. They prevent us from completing anything because they're always recruiting us to help them start something new. As a result, we create a slew of abandoned projects, hopes, and dreams (*all initially motivated by a sense of significance*). If you never finish, you're constantly being distracted by turtles.
- **Swordfish prevent us from stopping.** These distracting creatures push us to go faster and further than is appropriate, healthy, and sustainable (*motivated by achievement*). This obsession is never enough. There's never an end. Swordfish push us to keep going when it's time to slow down, stop, or pull back. Swordfish are the distractions that lead us to fulfill destructive behavior (*sometimes in pursuit of perfection*) slowly over time or in grand terrible moments.

Facing and embracing reality is no easy task, and the moment we overcome one distraction, another quickly pops up. **But, distractions only work because they offer us something we want or an outlet from what we don't want to face.**

The key to overcoming the first three distractions is clarity on our intentions (*purpose, vision, mission, and values*) while living fully committed to them. The vital step for overcoming the last is an articulated finish line and proper pacing for arrival.

The following chapters will continue to direct you towards what matters, so deflecting distractions is less challenging. When we get what we want, and fulfill our motivations in healthy ways, the distraction's power severely diminishes.

One of the most powerful ways to accomplish this is to embrace constraints and intentionally limit ourselves.

How Self Inducing Constraints Lead to Creativity & Innovation

Are you brave (*and disciplined*) enough to impose constraints on yourself to create the best possible business?

I'm taking small steps towards making movies (*directing and screenwriting*), and I recently had an exciting idea on how I could go about developing and honing my craft through self-imposed creative constraints inspired by a famous director's recent success in doing just this.

M. Night Shyamalan (*director of Sixth Sense, Unbreakable, & Signs*) rediscovered his filmmaking ability with the enormous financial success of Split in 2018 (*after several prior critical and commercial failures*). After watching an interview with the director[14], he discusses how he artificially constrained himself to move back to his strong storytelling roots.

Becoming a beginner again was his goal, and he stripped everything away that didn't foster the competitive edge, including funding the film himself. With less money to spend, tension and focus arose from owning every second and decision made. He only made money from the movie if it was financially successful. And, it required a great story to make that happen.

While M. Night had a large amount of movie-making experience, it eventually diluted the instincts that fostered his early success. Going into Split, he chose not to work with former team members. His new critical crew was on their first, second, or third movie. They were dangerous and instinctive, unclouded by an extended history of making movies. And this instinct fused with Shyamalan's experience created a fusion of something special.

With little time and money to make the movies, the project moved forward, and creativity exploded. It was precisely the ingredients required to spark the magic.

---

[14] Sway Universe Interview. 23 Jan. 2017. https://www.youtube.com/watch?v=voaaUeughDk

With a certified fresh rating from Rotten Tomatoes and $278 Million in the worldwide box office on a nine million dollar budget, Split was a monster success on all accounts.

Constraints are vital to fostering the quality required for success.

Let's dive into how these constraints can apply to your work, and how we reign back crazy work schedules to a healthy level.

Are You Working Every Day And All The Time?

Growing up, I was taught to take a day of the week to rest, release, and worship God. In Hebrew, it's called a Sabbath day (*and it goes with the Sabbath year*). It's so important; God gave it to Moses as one of the ten commandments (*yeah, I forgot too*).

> "Remember the Sabbath, and Keep It, Holy."

The first several years in Atlanta, I adhered to the principles of this legacy directive from my upbringing. As our marketing company journey progressed, I began taking more control of my destiny and trusting God less. When things got worse, I worked more. This workload was also a way for me to escape the things in my life; I did not want to face.

Unfortunately, when business would get better, I didn't cut back my workload, so the amount of time I worked grew over time. One Sunday turned to two Sundays, turned to every Sunday. Before I knew it, I was working every day and all the time. But, this road led to chaos, burn out, and a lousy existence.

This *"more"* approach was not working, so I prayed for a better way. Then, a friend reminded me of the weekly Sabbath and asked if I was honoring and practicing it in my life.

NO, I was not. And the effect was pronounced. Things were not getting done, and I was neglecting what mattered.

At that moment, I decided to take back my Sabbath and began down a road of working less and trusting God to do more (*the underlying principle behind the commandment*). While it seemed backward, life began to get better, and I became significantly more productive.

Within limited hours each workweek, I accomplish more in constrained time than I do working twice as many hours.

When I was working every day, and all the time, there was an incentive to procrastinate. I'd be working later, so I could do a task then instead of now.

But, by drawing a line in the sand, I either got it done, or it waited. This tension forced better planning and foresight to ensure I hit my goals (*more on that in a minute*).

A few years after pulling back my schedule, I had a client who was in the same spot working crazy hours. She was trying to do everything, but it wasn't enough. I asked her the following question.

> *"What if you did less, and trusted God to do more?"*

It was a profound question for her to ponder. And one required by us all. If you lack a belief in God, look at the data. Working over forty hours has diminishing returns (*as cited earlier*). Taking time off has practical benefits.

So, while structuring a hard boundary around my work sandbox may feel claustrophobic, it's one of the most freeing acts I've done.

What's something you're afraid of constraining?

Are you afraid to set a limit and work fewer hours? Are you concerned about charging a higher rate leading to less possible clients? Are you afraid to focus your business offering because it means saying no to numerous excellent opportunities?

Maybe now is your time to take a leap of faith and do something hard, not because circumstances require it, but because you want to foster the best you possible. Like it has for me, setting these boundaries could be the most freeing thing you do for yourself.

So, as my friend asked me, I'll do the same for you. Whether you believe in God or not, the research is quite clear that we humans need to pace ourselves and take regular time off.

Are you doing this weekly?

If not, maybe the following benefits will convince you.

How Planning Fosters Proactive Behavior

There's a simple (*and counterintuitive*) solution for those who excel with procrastination and struggle with proactive action.

Schedule time off. And, do it daily, weekly, monthly, and annually. It will foster proactive behavior today.

During the week, I start my workday at 8:30 am and end it at 6:00 pm. I don't work on Saturday or Sunday. For each month, I intend to take a few weekdays off (*which I've failed miserably at the past few years, but finally buckled down in 2019 to make it happen*). Every year, I also take a step back every December from blogging (*to provide a clear finish line and time to rejuvenate*).

When we schedule time off, we create boundaries and a sense of urgency that fuels productive behavior. It also encourages creativity.

I went from working every day and all the time, during the early Noodlehead Marketing years, to a block of 47.5 hours per week (*including lunch*). And yet, I accomplish way more than I ever did working crazy 70-80 hour work weeks.

So why is that? Why are we more effective with time constraints?

Several years into our Noodlehead Marketing journey, I had an essential team member who was leaving for an entire month traveling to another country. While we had many systems in place, she was the manager of what went on in the company. I wasn't sure how this month would go, so we both prepared the month before departure.

Metaphorically, I imagined there was a hurricane heading our way, and we needed to build up sandbags to protect us from the rising waters to come. So proactively, we did just that.

During this time, we communicated with clients, team members, and practiced many of the activities as we prepared for the upcoming change. When the time finally arrived for her to leave, we were prepared and equipped (*It also acted as a catalyst to improve and document our processes*).

When the month of her absence came, there were no issues at all. It was as if the hurricane waters came up to the first row of sandbags, but never touched the layers above. This preparation fostered a positive experience, and it allowed my departed employee to enjoy her time away. It was great to know we had over-prepared, but it was also great to know, had it been a bad storm, we would have been ready for it.

When we plan for time off and set boundaries, we'll get more done, have something to look forward to, improve our systems, and be ready for the worst outcomes (*productive paranoia*). If your goal is to perform at a high level, these are all benefits you'll want to foster.

Now back to you for some prodding.

Key Questions

- What's one step you can take today to start scheduling time away from work?
- What constraints will help you stay focused and perform at the highest level?

V. Manifest Your Transformation Outwardly

While a leader's transformation begins from the inside, it must manifest outwardly if a change has happened. This conclusion fosters an unsettling outward expression with the people and environments around us. It's troubling because change is scary, and how people respond is uncertain.

I recall at the end of 2010, after months of intentional outward living, life, and work got much harder. At this moment, there was a sense that I was facing deliberate opposition, consequences of my past, and a rising doubt, I chose the wrong path forward. It was at that moment when I truly felt enslaved to the business. Much like a Chinese finger trap, the more I struggled to escape its grasp, the more it latched onto me.

It's ironic how in these monumental milestones in our life, someone comes along needing help. By guiding them, we grow ourselves.

It was at this moment when a fellow entrepreneur was contemplating the shut down of her small business. Does she close shop or do the hard work to make it happen?

What was my response?

Figure out your individual vision (*define success*), mission (*how to get there?*) and purpose (*Why do it?*). Use that as your compass to decide what you do and how you do it.

My compass was telling me to serve and love others, not to have fear, to guide others to realize and actualize their visions and do it while maintaining my priority in Jesus, family, and work. And, to do these things despite the obstacles that came my way. These obstacles allowed me to demonstrate to others these traits more powerfully.

Be an example. Inspire others.

And, I've done this since then, as a small business owner, freelancer, blogger, and now in this book. Sharing my stories of failure and success, with the attached lessons learned helps you, and it teaches me.

A Year of Transformation

As I reflected on this moment several years later, the parable of the fig tree (*mentioned earlier*) came to mind.

> *And he told this parable: "A man had a fig tree planted in his vineyard, and he came seeking fruit on it and found none. And he said to the vinedresser, 'Look, for three years now I have come seeking fruit on this fig tree, and I find none. Cut it down. Why should it use up the ground? 'And he answered him, '****Sir, let it alone this year also, until I dig around it and put on manure. Then if***

> ***it should bear fruit next year, well and good; but if not, you can cut it down."*** *- Jesus of Nazareth*

Manure is used to fertilize the land. Fertilizing is the enrichment of soil for the production of crops (*fruit*).

When I look back at this moment, I see where I was being fertilized, enriched, cared for by God. Manure is waste, and it's not pretty. But, it has all the nutrients needed for growth and life.

When we cut down something; that's not working, we eliminate the opportunity for it to produce fruit. It's much wiser for us to wait to cut it down until after we've given it the attention required, and it still does not produce fruit.

This parable is a powerful visual for how we create an excellent environment for someone to grow, but ultimately, this only acts as a way to illuminate the heart of a person. A perfect setting does not create fruit-bearing people; it just allows them to grow fruit without hindrance (*and it gives leaders clarity when it doesn't*).

This quote from David Guzik's commentary encapsulates the sentiment well.

> *"The farmer, illustrating God, did not leave the tree alone. He gave it special care. Perhaps God is showing His special care for you right now — but it feels like there is manure all around you! Yet, don't resist God's work. Flow with it and bear fruit as He continues to work in your life." - David Guzik*

To your surprise, maybe there's something about **you** that needs changing. A blind spot, others easily recognize while you fail to notice.

Maybe your reflection in the mirror is not as great as you think. On that note...

What's It Like On The Other Side Of You?

It's been personally eye-opening for me to work with business owners as a freelancer since 2014 (*as opposed to how it unfolded when doing similar work as the owner of Noodlehead Marketing*).

I've now felt what it's like to be on the other side of business founders, especially as I witness how owners interact with their employees (*whom I am often interfacing with directly*) and me. And, this includes both positive and negative dynamics.

As a business owner, we have a tremendous amount of authority and control, and while we might mentally recognize how our words and actions affect people, we don't **FEEL** how it is to be those employees.

Working under the direction of several dozen owners, as a freelancer, has given me an abundance of first-hand involvement. It's acted as a mirror to help me experience how my many actions in this role previously impacted people who worked for me.

This mirror is a powerful reminder to keep a pulse check on those we lead, while also seeking out feedback from people regularly. It inspires me to act considerate, compassionate, and with understanding for the people I lead.

As leaders, it's not our strengths that derail us, it's our weaknesses.

> "When leading others, It's less about leveraging our strengths and more about managing our weaknesses." - Keith Eigel, Ph.D., Co-author of The Map: Your Path to Effectiveness in Leadership, Life, and Legacy

Years ago, I explored Strengthsfinder as a way to better understand myself and how to leverage my strengths. While that book steers us away from spending too much time working on deficiencies, Keith's comment illuminates how our weaknesses become self-sabotaging when we scale upward.

It's incredibly frustrating to feel like we're in the way of our success — many opt-out of making the jump because it means dealing with these pitfalls and weaknesses. Acknowledging and refining ourselves is hard, unpleasant, and scary.

To lead others in transformational ways for growing the business beyond our current capability requires placing ourselves at the mercy of others. Diving into the feedback of others, as well as our own, creates a visceral way for us to embrace this reality, learn, and have the motivation to grow.

Will you lean into the unpleasant tension or stay in your current comfort zone?

If you don't, you could find yourself causing an abundance of hurt with others.

Are You Using People To Achieve Or Helping Them To Develop Character?

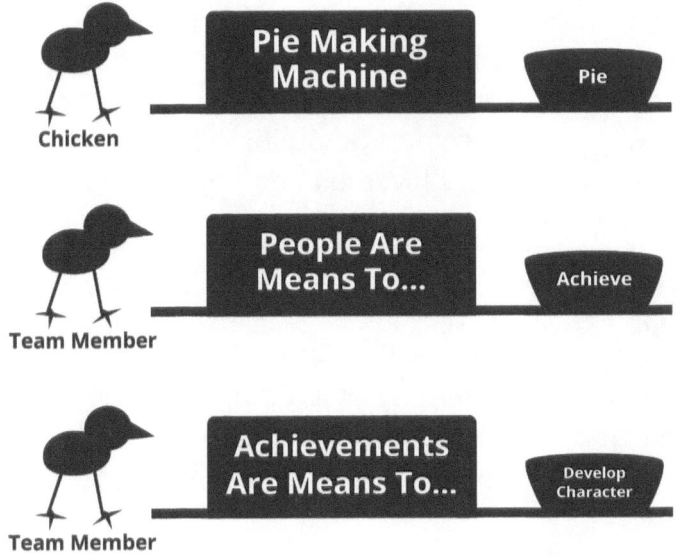

In the animated movie Chicken Run, the chickens are not producing enough eggs so the owner (*also the villain*), decides to buy a pie-making machine.

Chickens go in, and pies come out.

The owner believes this machine will turn her failing farm into a money-making machine (*and the chickens are terrified*).

As silly as it seems, it's a perfect visual for many entrepreneurs.

The Trap For Leaders

As a business owner striving for success, we easily fall into the trap of seeing our team members as the chickens in this metaphor. Team members go into our company, the pie machine, and out of it flows what we define as success or achievement; money, power, fame, or influence (*the pie*).

It's terrifying how easy we quickly fall into this dynamic.

In this mindset, the team is not a top priority, and we see them as a commodity, making it easy for us to burn them out knowing we can find someone else to take their place.

A Different Perspective

> *"Trying to Take Charge Strips You of Influence." - Jennifer Garvey Berger, Unlocking Leadership Mindtraps*

While seeking to achieve our goals and teaming up with others to do so is not itself a bad thing, the tension arises when the achievement and the relationship become at odds. It is these moments which quickly illuminate our order of priorities, and we learn whether success or people are our top priority.

Years back, I worked with a client (*referred to as Company A*). While working with them, I observed a high level of this achievement obsession.

There were situations where people in different ranks in the company were using each other as a means to achieve or accomplish their respective goals and less emphasis on character and relational growth.

Bob The Tornado owned Company A. He spent an abundance of time creating and accumulating a lot of great pies (*from the metaphor*). In his mind, these pies were part of his greatest achievements. His hard work and livelihood were in the' value of these pies.

He took a break from making these pies and went off to do other things. When he came back, some of his most prized pies were in a state of chaos, and others were creating new pies of different unwanted flavors

He was furious, and at that moment, he attempted to fix the broken pies and get rid of the new pies at the cost of the relationships with his team.

Fixing the mess was more important to him than the people he was hurting by fixing the mess, and it was at this point he revealed to the world that his achievement was more important than people.

When the team confronted him about this issue, he realized how his priorities were out of order and apologized for the way he acted.

From the perspective of the team, while BOB was gone, they spent time and energy creating their own pies. When BOB returned and started changing things, their immediate reaction was more about protecting themselves and their new pies and less about BOB as a person and their leader.

BOB was now in the way of what was important to them, and they wanted to get him out of pie making so they could continue making their pies without his disruption. When Bob confronted his team about the issue, they realized he had justifiable cause to be upset about the neglected pies, and they needed to all get on the same page about which pies they would make and how they would take care of them.

From my perspective, the issue was the same on both sides; it just looked different for both points of view. In the future, it would have been wise for BOB to follow the appropriate channels to communicate his frustration and concerns. For the team, it would have been wise to respond to the chaos with an intent to listen to BOB and deal directly with their interests.

Ultimately, in a messy kind of way, this all happened, but if one or both sides prioritized each other first, it would have played out with much less chaos and negative consequences.

How, For A Moment, My Dad Prioritized Achievement Above Our Relationship

Being on the receiving end of this performance-oriented dynamic has been a common trend in my life. Unfortunately, others have prioritized achievement above me, and this included my dad (*and now me, with my kids*).

My dad owned several package delivery routes, and in High School, I would help him install shelves and do maintenance on his business trucks. One time while I was helping him change the oil, I was not paying attention and let the oil drain out of the trucks onto the terminal floor.

It went all over the complex floor. Now while It was not as bad as the Deepwater Horizon oil spill, it was still bad. Oil was everywhere, and it was going to take all afternoon cleaning it up. As you can imagine, my dad was visibly upset, and he expressed this to me. From his perspective, his work was essential, and he was putting in a great deal of time. Now, I just added more work to his already heavy burden.

Being sensitive, I received his verbal chastisement personally. I didn't mean to do it, and I was more than willing to clean it up. I felt terrible enough on my own; I didn't need help feeling bad.

It was then I hoped he would have prioritized me above the work. I wanted to receive compassion and for him to come alongside and help me clean it up. When emotions settled, we did clean it up together, and he probably did most of the work, but the initial emotional outburst seared my soul (*unfairly to him*).

My dad never imagined how much this achievement dynamic in our relationship would have affected me for years to come, but thankfully, we reconciled over the years working towards a healthy relationship. And, the experience, among others, helped equip me to deal with task-oriented and demanding perfectionists.

Now the tension he faced is one I must address with my children as moments like these easily surface in my parental relationships. Knowing the pattern empowers me to curb the generational pattern in a new and better direction (*as my dad did with his father, and my kids will do with me*).

Priorities

People OVER **Achievement**

OR

Achievement OVER **People**

?

The Jump

What Matters Most?

In the Chicken Run movie, the owner's goal is to make more money. The chickens were a means to make that money. Is that a bad thing? Bob, the business owner, had the choice of firing his entire staff and hiring a new one. Why was that not the best course of action?

When it comes down to it, people matter, and our relationship with them is crucial. If you think about it as a bank account, one where you contribute and other times when needed, withdraw. Keeping a positive balance leads to less stress, higher levels of motivation, and the ability to take advantage of opportunities. And, as much as we don't recognize it at the moment, we reap what we sow. If we continuously prioritize achievement over people, we'll quickly find that people no longer want to be around or work for you (*even when you pay them a great deal of money*). Moreover, this argument doesn't dive into the moral implications or what we'd like others to do should the roles be reversed.

This insight and these stories are shared to help educate and inspire you to prioritize people above achievement in your life.

While this may be an issue we can learn and be aware of, it will likely be a lifetime tension we face. Maintaining priorities is hard, but being aware and accountable is a great step in minimizing its effect on our lives.

Cues For Keeping Our Priorities In Order

The following mental signals are helpful triggers for when priorities are out of order.

- When we feel people are "*in the way*" of our goal, this is a symptom our priorities are out of whack.
- When something goes wrong or disrupts us, and our first reaction is preserving our achievements instead of engaging with the person, this is a symptom; our priorities are off.
- When someone makes a mistake, and we are more upset about what it will take to clean it up than the relationship with the person, this is cause to think our priorities are out of balance.

Wise leadership requires moderation of how far we go. This insight is also true for those who are too nice; lacking assertiveness.

For these leaders, other lessons arise.

Can You Still Be Kind To Others And Succeed?

The saying goes; nice guys finish last, right?

Years ago, a friend expressed his frustration with being too nice in his business. Out of his niceness, he believed people took advantage of him, and he was beaten up by the world. This sentiment was one I related to deeply.

During our conversation, I saw what it was like to be on the other side of me when I was in the same hurt state. It brought back memories of when I asked myself if I could be successful and still be kind in the business.

I remember milestones in my journey where I had to go to dark places to survive and move forward with my life. There were team members and clients who preyed on me (*as I likely did with others*), and there was not a safe place to retreat.

There is a scene which comes from the 1995 film Casino, by Martin Scorsese, where they take a mob member to the cornfield, to a pre-dug hole. Unexpectedly, the surrounding mafia begins hitting him with baseball bats until he is just short of death. At this point, they throw him into the hole, where he is barely hanging on. It is at this point that they shoveled dirt on him, burying him alive.

In 2009, this was how I felt.

Everyone took their swing at me, and I was barely holding on, as the surrounding chaos buried me alive. I was helping others, doing my best, and nothing I did was good enough. I went to a dark place of despair.

As my friend was sharing with me, it reminded me of this season of my life. He was beaten up, and like me, he had turned his heart off to stop the pain. We both became a shell of who we once were.

So, how do we prevent ourselves from transforming from a nice, joyful, and loving person helping others into a cold, broken shell of a person? How do we treat others with kindness, not get beat up, and succeed at it?

While watching Mary Poppins[15], a concise answer came. Early in the film, Poppins is speaking to the father referring to his list of requirements in a nanny. One of his conditions is the nanny is nice, to which Mary Poppins replies, "**I am kind, but extremely firm.**"

Kind and firm, just as she stated it. It's when we are kind and not firm; we get ourselves in the most trouble.

Unfortunately, we live in a world where people are going to take advantage of us. Often, we do it to each other unaware while other times it's done intentionally.

Ideally, we are looking out for ourselves and those we interact with, but often this is not the case. When both people are not looking out for each other, it creates an opening for us to get hurt.

Deciding to stop being a kind person because people have been unkind to us is a tragedy. Doing so continues the cycle unkind people perpetuate. Instead, we ought to choose kindness, knowing there will be times when others treat us poorly.

Let's not have external forces define us, but instead, let's decide whom we want to be and how we want to respond. Let's also take responsibility and recognize it is likely our lack of firmness where we usually get hurt, not our kindness.

---

[15] Mary Poppins. Dir. Robert Stevenson. Perf. Julie Andrews, and David Tomlinson. Walt Disney Studios, 1964.

Using this insight as our mental foundation, here are three principles to help us to firmly enforce boundaries as we lead our family, team, and community.

1. Prioritize Values Above Needs

We all have our needs, and our situation is much like that of a mouse (*yep, another metaphor*). Mice need to eat to survive, and the mouse's appetite for cheese makes an excellent enticement for setting up a mousetrap.

The mouse has a legitimate need to eat, and as he goes for the cheese, the trap kills him.

Many times we get hurt after ignoring or missing multiple red flags that a trap is ahead. Being kind is sometimes the reason we miss the warning signs.

This scenario has played out for me with mentors, hiring people, finding clients, and working with vendors.

A toxic mentor entered my life after my wife, and I started a business and launched a political news website. Both of these ventures were new to me, and I had little clue about what we were doing.

Subconsciously, I knew I needed help, and when this person came along, I needed support, guidance, and counsel, to help navigate through the journey. He was also struggling in his life, and it was an opportunity for me to be kind and supportive.

Thinking I **needed** his help, and seeing his need were two problematic tensions I was unequipped to handle.

It opened me up to stay in an unhealthy relationship. It was also a catalyst to ignore the flags and compromise on my values to get what was needed. Other people were telling me about these flags, and I even acknowledged them. However, I believed I could receive the good and ignore the bad.

Now imagine the mouse from my earlier story dismissing the trap because he thinks he can get the cheese without setting it off. This sneaky arrogance and my lack of perspective and experience led to me getting caught. With limited perspective, I made this choice, and it cost me.

When it comes to filling our needs, it's essential we don't sacrifice our values and priorities.

2. Operating From A Mindset Of Abundance

> *"For the love of money is the root of all kinds of evil. And some people, craving money, have wandered from the true faith and pierced themselves with many sorrows." - Paul, the Apostle*

Another snag, which has caused me great grief, is operating from a mindset of scarcity instead of abundance. When we think and act in a way where we horde, we become more defensive of what we have, and we are more likely to settle for dirty scraps instead of a nice meal.

With my toxic mentor, there was a sense that I needed help, and finding it was hopeless. When it came to me, I grabbed and hoarded it because I didn't know if something better would come along later.

There were times when we hired the best of who was available to us even when they did not share or live out our values. When we sought clients, we accepted projects from organizations which did not align with our values, and with others who were not willing to work within our guidelines. Often, it was because we thought we needed the money, and getting paid became the most critical factor.

When we fear to lose the money, we allow others to treat us poorly. When we live with a mindset of enough, we are more likely to be firm in our interactions with others. It's another reason why debt can be so harmful.

3. Stop Being Kind As A Way To Avoid Conflict

Historically, conflict was a tension I avoided and fled. Tired, burned out and desiring a reprieve, I did not want to deal with the numerous realities we faced in my early years of entrepreneurship.

There were times when I was kind to a client as a way to avoid conflict, to keep the peace. In these cases, our kindness was a reaction to their disappointment, while other times, it was secretly done to avoid discussing a rocky issue.

When a client hired us for ten hours, and they ended up using fifteen, there were times when we ate the hours and called it kindness. But, this created a few different problems.

First, they usually did not know about our act of *"kindness,"* and second, we became resentful towards them when their unkind behavior would not change. It felt as if we would give, and those we were kind to would keep taking no matter how much we gave. It felt like whatever we did was never enough.

In these types of situations, we needed to lean in and deal with the conflict directly. It doesn't mean we are not kind or gracious, but when we learned to be accountable both ways, kindness became a more impacting and genuine gesture.

Lean Into Conflict, Master Firmness

We can be kind in business while dealing with others. Prioritizing our values above our needs, operating from abundance and leaning into conflict are three powerful ways we can be firm in our dealings with others. It is from this path where our kindness has the most impact on others.

Where are you kind in your business? Where do you need to be more firm with others?

As you learn to set and enforce better boundaries, we'll equip ourselves to lead others effectively.

Crab Mentality? Push or Pull? Two Insights For Leading People

If you've not heard the story of the crabs or the concept of *"crab mentality"* (*"if I can't have it, neither can you"*) here is a quick recap.

When people go fishing for crabs with a bucket, it's crucial they bring a lid for the first crab. The reason is that it attempts to crawl out of the bucket. Once you catch the second crab, you no longer have to keep the crab covered because the other crabs in the bucket will keep each other from crawling out.

When we are in the bucket (*a situation, trouble, etc.*) with others, we tend to pull each other down. Broken people have a hard time when others seek to leave their shared suffering or complaining. And instead of changing themselves, the entrenched workers prevent others from exiting. If they prevent others from escaping, they can continue justifying their misery and problems to themselves without taking responsibility.

Why do people who want out of the bucket resist so heavily when others offer them help?

Talking with my friend about this, he put his hand out and invited me to do the same. **He began pushing on my hand, and I immediately, out of instinct, pushed right back. He then put his hand out again, face up. I put my hand out, he grabbed it and began to walk away. I immediately began to follow.** These were very similar actions but resulted in two completely different responses.

When we push people to move forward, we foster resistance. If instead of pushing, we choose to open up, cast a vision, walk towards it, and invite others along the way, they're more likely to follow willingly.

A pull instead of a push could be just what you need to do.

Here are three ways to practically act this out in your small business.

Business Owners Dramatically Improve Their Company Culture By Doing These Three Things

Most business leaders don't realize how their actions and decisions affect other people. When we fail to act decisive, provide clear direction, and bring others along we're going to burn out our team, generate a slew of wasted efforts, and foster unhealthy conflict.

We must operate in a better way.

Since moving to Atlanta in 2005, I've worked directly with and under the authority of business owners. Working with founders, I've recognized the following three simple changes would move projects forward more effectively, while also building unity within their teams.

They are:

1. Acting Decisively
2. Providing Clear Direction

3. Bringing Others Along

When leaders don't do these things, it requires more time for all of us to get the work done, we're likely to spend more time and money to move items forward, and it causes unnecessary frustration. Many folks often are paralyzed by the lack of clarity, fearing their efforts will lack meaning.

Let's take a deeper dive into indecisiveness.

1. Act Decisively

My friend was recently having trouble with his website as a result of his hosting company. I too had issues with that same company, so I recommended two terrific hosting options. A few days later, I asked him which company he went with, and he said he didn't pick either. He spent too much time comparing the two options, and he just abandoned the project.

When we are not acting decisively, it results in us going around in circles. We go somewhere, but we go nowhere.

There was a company with a small team I worked with on occasion a decade ago. The owner would take us all to lunch. When we left, he'd inevitably ask everyone where they wanted to go to lunch. Lot's of *'I don't know,'* and passive comments soon followed. Since none of them were going to be decisive, I jumped into these conversations with where I wanted to eat. We ate where I wanted much of the time.

I recall many times running my business, where I found myself in between a rock and a hard place of decision making. I'd do research, talk with others only to realize **I was looking for a way out of my situation, not a real solution** to what I was facing.

When we get so caught up in analysis paralysis, we get stuck. I call this the **Dreamer** stage (*from The Island Story*). We think and plan, but we struggle to start.

It's not until the heat is hot enough (*the stick*) and the potential (*carrot*) is appealing enough that we'll make the jump from where we are to where we want to be.

When we have trouble making decisions with the small things, we're going to struggle significantly with the big important and hard ones. Sometimes, we're faced with two bad choices and must pick the better option. If you voted in the 2016 presidential election, you know how this feels.

Feeling and acting in uncertainty fuels anxiety, so if you struggle to act decisively, here are several questions to help you outgrow this shaky behavior unless you'd prefer to let fate decide by the flip of a coin.

> **Key Questions**
>
> - What do you hope/expect to happen after making your decision?
> - What will it cost you to make this decision? What will it cost you not to make it?
> - If you make the "wrong" decision, what will it cost you?
> - How difficult will it be to change course if you picked the wrong direction?

- Do you care more about perfection or progression towards excellence?
- When you look back in a day, week, month, year, or a decade, will you regret not acting?
- Are you willing to let what others think of you define the decisions you make?
- Is saving a few bucks worth all the time your spending making a decision?

These questions cover a range of motivations and fears that tend to drive indecisiveness. If any of these questions resonate with you, take a moment and write an answer.

While acting decisive puts us in a vulnerable place with other people (*who could quickly chastise us for the decision we make*), it makes life better and moves things along.

2. Provide Clear Direction

Imagine I came to you seeking to purchase multiple commercial properties and you present me with several options. I proceed to tell you I do not want any of them and provide no feedback as to why not. I also don't give any feedback on what I am looking for, even after your persistent prodding.

You're now shooting in the dark, trying to figure out the next group of properties to present me. But no matter how skilled you are, it'd require a string of good luck to land on showing me the right set of options.

Feedback matters, and it matters most from the owner of a company.

Many business owners ask their team to deliver on projects those of which they have no clarity. And their team does the best job they can to deliver, only to fall short time and time again. They'll get a typical response that what they've provided is not right, but the owner can't say why not.

> *"I'll know it when I see it,"* they say.

Sometimes these owners are not spending the time to think through their intentions. They're too busy, or they're lazy. Other times, they don't know what they want, and they're not willing to wait and figure it out before starting the project.

It's the owners who expect so much, give so little, and get so frustrated and angry after the fact, that upset me the most.

The key to overcoming and excelling at providing clear direction is answering five questions.

Why, where, how, within, and what's at stake?

They all help us determine our intent. While we may not have a concise answer to these questions, we should at least answer them when we're asking others to drive our ideas and projects forward.

3. Bring Us Along

Observing my client's employee speaking to his superiors, I noticed a communication failure. A few weeks prior, they had all agreed on a direction for their strategic sales efforts, and this sales rep had moved forward from that decision. Unfortunately, the owner decided on a new course in a follow-up meeting unbeknownst to this employee.

They went a different direction, but they failed to communicate this change with the team member impacted by this decision. While he was okay with the change, he was frustrated by the lack of communication and the fact that no one brought him along.

I'd love to say this is a rare occurrence with small business owners, but no, it happens quite often. I recently came up with a game plan with another client for a marketing project. I moved forward only to find out from another team member he decided to move in a different direction, and never told me. Again, I didn't have an issue with the change in the decision, but it was frustrating to be left in the dark, wasting my time on a canceled endeavor.

If you're a business owner, and you make a choice or change your decision, it's your responsibility to disseminate this information to your team and bring them along. If you don't, you'll foster frustration and wasted efforts.

The next time you make a change in direction, think about who will be affected and communicate with them what changed and why. You'll be left with a happy and motivated team instead of a frustrated and angry one (*keep the relational bank account full!*). Business owners who build loyalty and positive work experiences foster a healthy culture.

Practice acting decisively, clarifying expectations, and communicating thoroughly with your team. When you master these three habits, you'll set the foundation for your team, department, and organization for years to come.

A New And Better Business Requires A Transformed Founder

> *"If we want to change our organization, we've got to start by changing ourselves."* - Dr. Keith Eigel

Whether it's directly the case or not, you must accept responsibility for the state of your small business. It is because of you that the company remains stuck. And, it will always regress to your ceiling of competence. So, unless you change, nothing else will. Your frustration will play out perpetually, and it'll become a state of hell for you, and those in your orbit.

Your first step forward is acknowledging this reality, your responsibility, and moving through the process, not just to pay lip service, but to fundamentally go on a journey to change for the better. The goal is to see yourself as others do. To know who you are, not how you ideally perceive yourself. Get the raw words from those around you, about what it feels like being on the other side of you.

Growth By Learning Along The Way

"Pain + Reflection = Progress" Ray Dalio, Principles

Do the hard work.

Lean into your discomfort, and learn through it. Embrace the power of aligning with others, the assurance of self-authoring from the inside out, and be willing to let go of your way of thinking and doing.

It's your mission to stop yourself from reacting and interacting with others in the way you always have. Pause, reflect and choose how you'll respond in a way that aligns with your personal vision of whom you want to be. What you're weakest at, and the things you avoid like the plague, are likely the very details you must lean into to illuminate your pitfalls.

Moreover, it would help if you took not only a personal responsibility but also invite external accountability. Be honest about your struggle, and where you need to change.

Two Paths Forward (*But Really Only One*)

Your two choices are to either embrace or resist this change. The longer you resist, the harder and more severe your fall will be when things unravel. Unless you want to be a hermit for the rest of your life, this is not the path for you.

Embrace change now, and from a humble heart, you'll benefit from a rich growing experience. It'll be scary as you face the terror of within, and from your past. You'll have to look at the parts of you that are decaying and broken. You'll no longer be able to live under the illusion that you're a magnificent, wonderful person worthy of people following you to the ends of the earth (*Yep, it's time to do major surgery on your narcissism*).

Broken, and contrite, you'll feel vulnerable, but you'll also have an excellent opportunity to step up and lead those around you from a new and better foundation. And, you'll be more thoughtful and wiser as you lead them towards a clear and focused destination.

Accept your limitations, embrace your fear, grow through your weakness, and choose the neglected path forward.

It is this step that is most important. Steps two, three, and four are critical for the jump, but they are also a series of tests to further enforce this one. Without this personal transformation, none of the others will lead to your goal.

There are no shortcuts.

7. Step Two - Build A Strong Business Foundation

In the parable of the two builders (*one wise & the other foolish*), the first builds upon a rock foundation while the other upon the sand. When the storms came, the wise builder's house stands up strong while the foolish builder's property is destroyed.

A simple metaphor with profound implications for how we start the construction of our business. How equipped, prepared, and trained we owners are to handle storms dictates how we build. I've experienced life with sandy foundations, and the ensuing chaos is traumatic and costly.

I wrote the following section for those who want to establish the type of business foundation that will last the most severe storms. It's not always the most exciting of tasks, but it's the most critical process for anchoring our business deeply into bedrock.

Our starting point is discovering what we have to work with today.

What If The Thing You're Looking For Is Right In Front Of You?

In 2012, my company was homeless as the result of our office flooding and the landlord not addressing the issue.

A local Norcross, Georgia church generously offered to let us use their location since they didn't use it during the week, and using the space would result in more income for the landlord. It was a win-win, but we went into it knowing it was a temporary solution.

While the new office worked out well, the team was anxious to move along and land in our final destination. As we talked about what we wanted, I realized the things we were seeking were quite similar to what we had in this temporary home.

However, the team didn't see this the same way, so I pulled us all into a room and asked questions about our ideal office. We listed out these attributes on the whiteboard in my intentional attempt to help them discover **the very office they were looking for was the actual office we were currently using.**

After we finished describing it, I asked, *'what changes would we need to make for our existing office to become the ideal one?'*. Then, they realized with only a handful of superficial changes to our existing setup; we'd have the office we were seeking. We wouldn't have to move, and the cost would be a fraction of what it'd be anywhere else.

Ironically, what we wanted was right in front of us.

What about with you? Do you have a person you wish would work for you? What about a vendor or partner company? What about a place you'd like to have or an elusive solution to your chronic problems?

It is possible you're so busy looking for the thing you want that you've missed what's actually in front of you?

It may feel like the grass is greener elsewhere, but with a little work, we can have the same yard and prevent the ruining of another green yard.

It merely starts with the foundations of every business.

Intentions.

Business Intentions

While clarifying our intent may be a significant step to take before we start, the reality is that most of us dive into things without thinking it through. If you've thoughtlessly gone into business ownership without understanding your intent, now is the time to stop and reflect on it.

This audit is where we'll learn if we ought to stay or change paths. Defining what we want and why we're doing it equips us to see how we most effectively traverse the path.

While this may seem like a waste of time, it is the hard discovery work here that keeps us anchored when we want to panic.

Before we turn to the Formula for Intentionality to help us get grounded, let's explore why intentionality matters, **especially in an ocean of competitors.**

When Building Your Business, Why & How You Build It Matters

How do the countless companies stand out from the crowd in a meaningful way?

It comes down to knowing the **vision** you have for your customer, deeply understanding **why** you've built the company, and having **a plan** to live out this purpose.

So, how do you best discover the vision for your customer? It requires a history where you've walked in the shoes of (*or spent significant time with*) your client, so you know the pain points and challenges in an intimate way. It requires the vision to understand how to overcome those challenges.

In my journey to freelancing full-time, I discovered a team who built a company with this type of clarity. The name of this technology startup is Harpoon. They help studios, agencies, and freelancers succeed by leading their new customers through a process to answer and define pivotal aspects of their business (*financial goals, planned revenue, intelligent billing, & controlled expenses*).

Practically speaking, Harpoon tracks financial progress and manages invoices, and it's terrific. It does a bit more than just those things, but those two things alone have aligned so closely with how I approach my work, it's as if they pulled a chapter out of my freelancing book (*Path of the Freelancer*) to create the software!

I was immediately intrigued by their messaging and approach. Harpoon knows that invoicing is a tool, but what we users need is a plan. They've got a page dedicated to their methodology, and I was impressed.

Whether we realize it or not, any tool we use pushes us into a framework or methodology, but few companies walk us through and communicate it so explicitly.

The financial software I was using for the previous eighteen months started with the intent to empower small business owners and freelancers by making it easy to manage invoices and finances. It had a similar origin, but unfortunately, the founders sold the company. As it usually happens in a transition like this, things and motivations changed priorities. While the new owner support continued, they purchased the company with the intent to build a new financial tool and migrate all users over to it.

Now facing an impending transition to a new financial tool, I could either switch over to the new one created by the new owner or I could switch over to the intriguing Harpoon.

Much more deliberate than I used to be, I opted to explore both options over a few months. I'd select the option which best aligned with my values and approach. I reached out to the existing company to explore their new tool and at the same time, signed up for a trial of Harpoon. These actions were both followed by a series of communications with both parties about my intent to switch over. I wanted a fair comparison.

The new tool, from the new owner, functionally served all the needs I'd have as a freelancer. It also offered the ability to make taxes and payroll easy. Functionally speaking, it'd be a great tool and a likely upgrade from the system I was using.

While using Harpoon's trial, I fell in love with the framework of the system they built. While setting up the account, the system walked me through the foundational steps (*Set a goal, plan revenue, invoice intelligently, & control expenses*). Since I had already worked through these steps before I considered Harpoon, I wrote in my answers, and the tool prepared the system around my goals.

Harpoon not only made their financial tool simple and easy to use, but they also set it up in a way that leads the users to make crucial decisions that will set them up for success and increase the likelihood of achieving their goals.

It was at this point that I realized how much the approach of a company matters. Their method is driven by why they do what they do, and their vision for what they want for their clients.

Both tools had the functionality I needed, but it wasn't a functionality comparison that brought me to Harpoon. It was how Harpoon uniquely tailored their app's interface around my context of freelancing as a consultant and marketer. They designed the tool for me without ever having known me. It was a surreal and unique experience.

With Harpoon, I've found not just a tool to help me forecast and plan my freelancing business, but I've established a business partner that will run alongside me.

As we move forward together, I expect the evolution of their tool will continue to foster the type of approach that continues to empower my freelancing success.

When you build your business, you want to create something that will profoundly impact your target customer.

We'll explore a process to help you do this, but before we do, I'd like to dive into a massive failure while running my previous business to illuminate the opposite scenario of what I've just described.

A Failed Project Gone Terribly Wrong

In the fall of 2010, I came face to face with a Sheriff. I was sitting down at my office desk when I looked over to see an officer in uniform enter. My eyes immediately darted away as my mind ran through numerous scenarios of why he was there. Bracing for the worst-case scenario, I turned away, hoping he wouldn't see me.

During our previous year, we spent a significant amount of time discovering what values our company would embrace. Two of these values were excellence and accountability, and this situation was about to test them both.

The Sheriff was there to serve a notice. Our project had gone terribly wrong, and our client was suing Noodlehead Marketing for almost fifteen thousand dollars. In trying to downplay this event with the team, I quickly signed for the notice and continued working. I did not want anyone to panic or worry, so I blindly hoped my employees had not noticed this encounter.

My mind continued to spin and spiral, and it was clear that I could not avoid my mistakes any longer.

To find the answer, I had to rewind twelve months earlier, to 2009. Our sales were down, and our expenses were up. As the team grew, the burden increased, and our monthly break-even point was climbing higher and higher. Many of our client's projects were on hold, and with Christmas around the corner, I did not want to tell our team, or my wife, we were short on funds for processing payroll.

Then, what seemed like a gift from heaven, came a project to bridge the gap and keep us chugging along. From a sales point of view, it was a slam dunk as we were charging much less than our competitors. It was one of the easiest sales we ever made.

Unfortunately, the economic tension we were facing made it hard to review the situation objectively. It was a project outside our wheelhouse, and our decision to take the project ended up being a costly mistake. We were not equipped to deliver with excellence, and we were not ready to handle the demands of the customer.

Because of the difficulty of this project and the client, we could have increased our chances of success if I led and managed the project and if we hired experienced external resources to execute the tasks. Unfortunately, we needed the money which left us unable to engage the external resources. Deep down, I knew this would end poorly, and so I distanced myself from the impending train wreck.

As expected, it was a challenging project with a demanding client. Our team was underpowered, and I put more and more distance between the client and myself.

Our incompetence and the client's domineering attitude made for a nasty soup. They paid us around fifteen thousand dollars, and at a certain point of not making enough progress, they pulled the plug and asked for their money back. We went back and forth debating, which led to lawyers getting involved.

We built the contractual scope, but we had verbally set expectations above and beyond what our contract stated, and we could not deliver.

By the letter of the law, we could have defended ourselves, but in my heart, I knew we had to face the situation head-on and pay for the consequences of our poor decision-making.

It took time and extreme pressure, but our core values of excellence and accountability (*with the weight of a lawsuit*) pushed us to face reality and make things right. A day before they filed the case in court, we agreed to reimburse them the money they paid.

When we started the project, we thought the money would help us. After reviewing the cost of paying the team, lawyers, and reimbursing the client, we came to realize; we were in a much worse situation than before. Not having the money to pay the client back, we thankfully agreed to a generous payment plan over the following two years.

We realized, our financial stress led us down a series of poor decisions as we ignored warning flags, so we could get what we thought we needed. It was like we were hungry mice who lacked cheese (*remember the metaphor?*), and we were so hungry we chose to eat the cheese inside the mousetrap (*regardless of the potential consequences*).

The first time Noodlehead Marketing fell into debt came as a result of us grabbing hold and not letting go of something we wanted. In this situation, we ended up in debt because we grabbed hold of what we thought we needed to pay our bills.

There are situations we face where we feel like we have to settle, compromise our values, or do something we believe will end badly because of the pressure we feel.

In these situations, I've chosen to do what is right and trust God for his provision. I won't take what seems like our only option (*when it's a terrible one*). Otherwise, we make bad decisions, indirectly leading us to do the very thing we committed not to do!

Let's commit to lean into conflict and address it as early as possible. Let's commit to being humble, admit we are wrong, and do what we can to reject passivity and take responsibility.

Our commitments will minimize how we hurt each other and maximize our success in work.[16] The best way forward from this scenario is starting strong.

How A Stable Foundation Fosters Growth & Prosperity — And How We Must Eliminate The Opposite Approach

> *"The Role Of A Leader Is To Amplify Good And Dampen Stress."* - Doug Shipman

Hand your kids a box of Legos and tell them to build a tower. As they're making it, take away half their blocks including ones they've already used to create it.

A few minutes later, instruct them to limit their color use, even if they've used some of those colors in their construction. Wait a few minutes, and tell them to take

---

[16] Explore how we should have responded to this project gone terribly at JasonScottMontoya.com/jump

their tower downstairs and build it there. While they're carrying it, try and knock them down and tell them not to let the tower break.

How well do you think they'll do at completing their project?

Not good and the problem is not them, it's you.

When it comes to building a department or business, this no-plan reactive approach is often how entrepreneurs interface with their team.

In my scenario, it's obvious how harmful it is to grow, how frustrating this "style" is to the creator, and ultimately how problematic it is for accomplishing our objectives (*I'm guilty of leading people in such a frustrating way*).

Stability and coherent, consistent direction are foundational for building something worthwhile. And, for providing safety for someone to create something meaningful over the long-term.

Planning prevents these mid-stream changes from negatively affecting the construction. But, it's not until we know, feel, and experience this pitfall that we as leaders are willing to change our approach. To operate proactively, and to provide room for our team to build is a gift of empowerment.

Always being given new missions or having the rug pulled out from underneath us will consistently lead to low morale and poor results. So if we do finish the mission, we'll burn people out along the way.

How is your negative reactive behavior harming your team's ability to grow your business?

Once we choose to operate with a robust and unmoving foundation and proactively lead with consistency, we're forced to face the underlying problem causing this harmful behavior.

Commitment to one mission and deciding to say no to everything else (*yeah, focus is a common theme in this book*).

This decision and our follow-through are how we...

Build From A Position of Strength

Chasing business scalability is a slippery path. When we focus solely on the scale, we lose sight of what matters for growth. Losing sight means never attaining the size we seek.

The key to successful scalability is how we start and the initial structural integrity.

During the early part of the Noodlehead Marketing journey, I recruited team members before I could genuinely afford to do so. While it would have been better to maximize our capacity and create a queue of future clients, I didn't choose this path. Thus, the only way I could justify keeping these team members was through constant client acquisition.

After achieving moments of success, the daunting task

of doing it all over again at the start of each month persisted (*our unexpected debts made it worse*). The times of feeling ahead were slim to none.

This situation describes building a business from a position of weakness.

As we progressed, the need for more paying clients led to shortchanging ourselves and sacrificing the margin required to deliver well and get ahead. We sought to provide sales deals (*to our detriment*) to land business faster out of fear and inexperience. Eventually, we slipped into a cycle of robbing Peter to pay Paul. And before we knew it, we were playing catch up, to survive.

This approach was not a wise way to live or operate a business. While this cycle could have continued, we had a client generously fire us in a way that gave us the margin we needed to shift the dynamic. And this milestone forced us to face the reality of what it took to sustain the business we created.

Adapting to Our Weaknesses

This downward spiral was driven by only considering the tip of the iceberg, not the entirety of what was required. Our unrealistic beliefs perpetuated the inevitable.

> "Truth is the essential foundation for producing good outcomes." - Ray Dalio

When we face the truth and respond accordingly, we set the foundation required for actual growth and long-term scalability.

Let me illustrate what it looks like to pursue a vision while also embracing reality along the way.

As a business, there will be times when we deliver goods or services, and unfairly don't get paid. Regardless of how well we seek to minimize this reality, we won't be able to eliminate the possibility. So, we need to plan as if it'll happen.

When we don't plan, we'll scramble to make up for it when negative unexpected events inevitability happen. For this possible scenario, we'll want to charge enough across all customers that when one client does not pay, it does not affect our operations.

Yes, not getting paid will be painful, but at least it won't affect our ability to fulfill our commitments.

In 2016, three different clients failed to pay me for my services. Unfortunately, three-thousand dollars (*2.6% of my annual 2016 income*) went into the abyss. However, with generous cash flow in tandem with my yearly income, this did not negatively impact our lives. It only slowed down our ability to save for a house downpayment and shrink our debt.

Now Strong As A Solopreneur

In my freelancing business, the approach is to maximize my foundations and build on them. And, it's to establish justification (*demand and margin*) before existence instead of after it. As a freelancer, this means cultivating a robust and full book of business.

As a result, I've increased my rates every year to deal with the demand increase and accelerate my financial goals. When I hit my capacity, I refer my clients to other freelancers, while project managing and directing my client's other contractors.

With a full plate of business, I'm perfectly positioned to grow a marketing agency from a strong, scalable foundation hiring talent and delegating the work. Since I'm not interested in creating another marketing company, I continue to increase my rates and build virtual teams to execute the work.

This approach allows me to work fewer hours, manage less responsibility, and earn more income. It's a model that enables me to write this book and pursue my desire to become a financially viable author.

Build Pillars of Strength

There are countless ways to build from a position of strength, and another example is us minimizing our debt. In 2018, we finished paying off our 2017 Kia Sedona auto loan and shifted the focus of our surplus cash towards paying off the remainder of our student loans in 2019.

By minimizing our financial debts, our position of strength increases, providing us additional margin and leverage to live generously and wisely.

When you reflect on your business, do you find you've positioned yourself and your organization from a place of strength? Alternatively, do you consistently find yourself playing catch up merely to survive?

Now is an excellent time to shift the dynamic to a strong foundation.

Setting The Foundation Right Using The Formula For Intentionality

To help us move away from building on shaky foundations and towards bedrock anchored endeavors, we'll explore the blueprint for our business foundation using the Formula For Intentionality.

With intent, we make a choice. So what are the many little choices contributing to the larger one?

The Formula provides us with the insight we need to define and refine the elements that make up our intent.

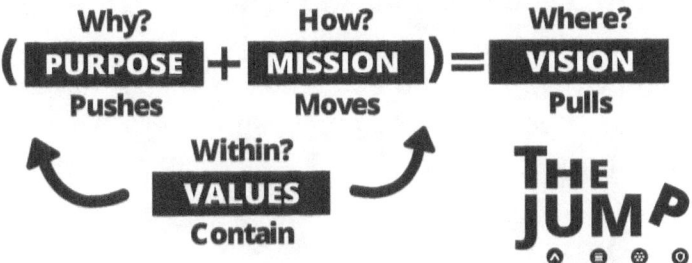

Purpose plus mission, within a set of core values, equals our vision. These ingredients give us specific questions to attain our intent.

Purpose is our "*why.*" It's our most relevant and vital belief for the business. This belief launches us forward, and it gets us out of bed every morning to do it again.

Mission is our "*how.*" It's how our company will live out its purpose. Mission moves us along and keeps us from stagnating.

Our **core values** are the **guidelines** we choose to operate "*within*" as we live from our purpose and live out our mission. They help contain and direct our activities and mindset day-to-day.

Vision is our "*where.*" It is the destination we believe we'll end up, and the results arriving with us. Vision pulls us to the finish line when nothing else will, and we feel like giving up.

Living our mission from purpose within our core values results in a vision. If we find ourselves living this out and the vision is different, we'll need to adjust another element of our formula, since intentions don't always reflect reality.

For us to test out an idea, we need a purpose. For us to move it forward, we need a mission. For us to stay on track, we need values. And finally, for us to finish, we need a compelling vision, one with which we are fully committed.

Personal Intentions

My personal purpose is to embrace the life of Jesus Christ (*the life he lived and the life he gave*) with a responsive mission of sharing this life. I operate within the guidelines of love, mindfulness, openness, and accountability. The result of this type of living is a state of thriving together, my vision.

While succinct and clear, these personally meaningful statements are the product of years of defining and refining. While difficult, it is incredibly rewarding to dive deep inside ourselves and recognize our intentions.

I house my freelancing, entrepreneurship, and all creative endeavors inside these written directives.

For example, I steward my client relationships well because I believe it lives out my purpose. I share on my blog because it fosters my mission. And when my work, project, or community endeavor lacks intentionality, my personal intentions fill the gap and motivate me forward.

Once we know and articulate our intentions, we have the power to change them, and this formula helps us get there effectively. I've tweaked and updated my personal intentions for years and you will too.

As we traverse these individual elements of the formula in the following sections, we'll primarily focus on it in the context of our company's intentions. I encourage you, as part of becoming a better leader, to define and articulate your personal intentions. They'll give a strong foundation for the business you seek to create.

What's Our Company Purpose?

The reason we choose to start a business is an important one. Because our efforts are launched from it, it's the most important first step we should take.

The healthiest purpose is one which intrinsically values business ownership and the entailing reality. If running a company is an outlet to avoid all other options, we are setting ourselves up for failure.

Let's dive deeper into purpose and how it works.

What Is Purpose?

As mentioned earlier, purpose is our '*why*.' **It is our most important belief, and it pushes us forward.** Purpose provides the energy and excitement to start an idea we've newly discovered.

Purpose is why we get up in the morning instead of staying in bed. It is why we choose to continue living. It illuminates the meaning of our lives. When all else fails, and we have lived with purpose, we have succeeded at what matters most.

Is there an idea you have thought about doing but have yet to start? A product, a service, a book?

The reason we don't start is the lack of a committed purpose. We lack the why, a belief about a fundamental truth. When we find purpose in our project, the inherent motivation launches us forward.

If there's something you wish to start, spend the time to discover the idea and its benefits to help you find a purpose worth launching.

Once you find it, be warned, having a purpose is a powerful motivator and requires discipline to harness its full potential. The passion from purpose launches us forward quickly.

Visionaries have an abundance of purpose, and they tend to launch many ideas and projects. Unfortunately, without considering the larger picture, visionaries start so many projects (*or companies*) they are not able to finish any of them. Their overcommitment paralyzes them.

In other cases, they launch the idea, and after it gets stale and the passion fades, so does the project. They abandon it and move on to the next idea, not finishing what they started. Over time, they leave a trail of unfinished work.

For Noodlehead Marketing, our purpose was to be an example of excellence and accountability.

If this was the only thing we could be to each other and our clients, we considered it a success, even in the context of project failures.

Here are other organizational purpose statements.

- Positively impact the lives of others (*CablesAndKits.com*).
- Inspire happiness (*Dragon Army*)
- Inspire and nurture the human spirit (*Starbucks*)

- Connect people to what's important in their lives through friendly, reliable, and low-cost air travel. (*Southwest Airlines*)
- Helping people on their path to better health. (*CVS, which is why they don't sell tabacco*)

There are countless others. Take a moment, and Google the purpose of your favorite companies. These examples give you inspiration and ideas as you shape your own.

What Is Your Purpose For Entrepreneurship?

Are you choosing to start and run a company because you want to generate a higher income?

Entrepreneurship does not guarantee this. In fact, for many, it could lead to a lower income or none at all.

Are you choosing to run a business because you can't stand working for someone?

Many of the issues we struggle with while working for someone tend to get amplified when we're responsible for a team and clients.

Are you founding a company because you're running away from particular types of problems?

Running away from problems and towards entrepreneurship will lead you to those same challenges, likely exaggerated.

To succeed, we need to be sure our purpose is in alignment with our vocational direction. This *"why"* will push us to get up in the morning, push us through difficulty, and is the foundation to create the life and work we want. If money is the driver, we'll eventually cave into the weight of merely surviving.

If you're running away from something, you may end up face to face with that very terror. You need something to inspire you to greatness, not just a fear of the consequences from failure.

My Personal Motivation For Business Ownership

It wasn't until I concluded my marketing business in 2014 that I fully recognized my personal motivation for launching the company. **Ending important things in our life has a way of bringing us back to the beginning, to that launching purpose** (*even if it wasn't externally articulated*).

Before I ever launched the business, I wanted to direct movies. Yeah, the ones you see in the theaters and rent for home watching. Inspired by Steven Spielberg's story, I created videos and animations during and after high school. Once I graduated, I wanted to go professional.

But my problem, stemmed from poor strategic decisions, was that instead of getting a degree in filmmaking, I got one in animation because I learned it before college and thought it would be the easiest way to graduate college (*which I didn't want to do, but out of honor for my father's request, did*).

I believed the influence and affluence from my entrepreneurial success would enable me to pursue my dream. It turned out not only did my decisions take me away from my dreams, but it also contributed to relational neglect of my God, my wife, and my community.

Firmly convinced I was going to make a positive difference through the entertainment industry, I lost sight of my priorities as my way of doing things took me the opposite direction. Forcing my dreams to happen cultivated chaos in my life.

Halfway through the business journey, I recognized something was off and grounded the business in its purpose and vision (*the one I shared earlier*). It became the business I would run if I were to choose a marketing agency as my vocational path.

In the final year of operations (*during the Sabbath year*), I was asking myself if I would choose a marketing company if I were to start over vocationally. The answer was no.

Without a personal reason for continuing the company, it meant I needed to end it, even though our team, mission, work, and clients were terrific (*and because it was too small to sell*). As painful as it was, I chose to walk away from something good.

Our business should serve a distinct purpose for its own sake but also for our life as well.

How does this vehicle (*business*) take us (*and others*) to the destination? Those that share our end game make a reliable partner on the team.

But, I had to dive deep and explore what was going on inside me. Defining success was part of the journey.

This One Thing Helps Us Stop Wondering If We're Failing

When we don't know if we're failing or succeeding at something, we feel like a failure. We could be giving great effort and making progress but still, feeling poorly.

But, there's a simple action to stop feeling this way.

Define success.

When we know what it means to succeed, we know when we're succeeding or failing. We no longer wonder, we know. Knowing allows us to respond.

With my freelancing work, I've defined weekly success by the number of paid hours logged. My target is 30.8. At the end of the week, this number lets me know if I succeeded or failed. If I failed, I change my actions for the following week to achieve the goal. If this failure negatively affected someone else, I apologize and make it right (*as appropriate*).

This definition of success is also part of our vision. We'll explore that in a moment, but first, let's examine two options for how small business success can manifest.

What Is Success For Your Business? Here Are Two Options

> *"If you can't communicate your vision and you can't connect with people, you're going to have a really difficult time as a business leader being successful."*
> *- John C. Maxwell*

During the years at Noodlehead Marketing consulting with numerous business owners, I quickly realized three crucial insights.

First, people fail to define personal intentions. Second, they fail to define their company's intentions. And lastly, they fail to align the two together (*impossible to do when neither exists*).

It's useful to see our business as a vehicle so that we can overcome these pitfalls. Is it taking us towards our destination? The primary reason I shut down my marketing company was that the vehicle was taking me away from my personal destination. It was going in the opposite direction of what I valued and sought.

Business doesn't always have to be about setting up scalable systems, growing large, and taking over the world (*although that is one of them*).

There's another option.

I've been working with a client over the past few years where I've consistently asked him what type of business he wants to create (*something I ask most of my clients*).

Does he want to build a scalable business model so he can grow large and do great things on a grand stage or does this owner wish to sustain a small business that allows him to live the life he wants while employing a handful of people nearby (*or none at all*)?

Driven by my desire for influence and affluence, so that I could pursue my ambitious endeavors, I sought to build and grow a larger organization.

I also believed that running a business would get easier as it grew. It turns out; it's the opposite. More team members, more clients, equals an increase in responsibility (*and complexity*).

In many cases, our company can take us away from what we love. For me, it did.

A Lifestyle Business

What is this other option? Start by defining what type of life you want to live and what income is required for you to live that life. From there, create a business that allows you to sustain that lifestyle in a positive and meaningful way.

As a freelancer, that's what I've done. In 2017, I hit my top tier annual income goal, and in 2018, I sustained it. After aggressively shrinking our debt, I'll diversify earned income, not just among multiple clients, but through publishing books and creating other products (*such as courses*).

There's a sweet spot where our income far exceeds our obligations, and our revenue comes from multiple sources. It's one with less stress and an abundance of margin — a life of peace and generosity.

Defining the finish line before you start makes it easier to deflect distractions and accelerate the journey. It also makes it more likely you'll create the type of business you want. These examples provide fodder as you wrestle with the vision for your small business.

What Is Your Vision For Business Ownership?

How would you describe your business where it was successful in every way you imagined? And how will it facilitate your personal goals?

In answering this question, you'll find vision.

Without vision, you'll wander. Although, if your goal is to explore and learn new things, wandering may be a good thing!

For those of us with families and obligations, we don't quite have that luxury. Reflect on your context when working through this process. The clearer we see what we want, the more focused we become in moving towards this focal point.

So, what does our life look like both personally and professionally once we have arrived at our destination?

Before we answer, let's dive deeper into explicitly understanding vision.

What Is Vision?

Vision is our **WHERE**.

It is where we believe we will find ourselves at the end of a particular journey. It's what we ultimately want.

Vision pulls us forward. It is the doorway of what we see at our destination. It is the world created from living out our beliefs.

Vision is what pulls us forward when feelings, thoughts, and others are telling us to quit. It is what we hope for that keeps us going, and it includes those of which we care.

Is there something you've quit?

A business?

A marriage?

A dream?

The reason we don't finish is a lack of vision. We lack the belief (*and associated discipline*) that we can overcome obstacles to get to our destination.

If you want to finish, discover your vision.

It is in our dark times and challenging obstacles we need faith in our end goal. To sacrifice the immediate to gain the long-term requires vision. Without it, we settle for short-term wins at the cost of our future.

Vision is a powerful force. With a focused and clear vision, we become achievers. We do what is necessary to get where we're going. **When we face obstacles we don't wonder if we should continue, we instead think of how we'll overcome.**

My personal vision is, Thriving Together. This vision is what pulls me forward when chaos is around me. When brokenness and isolation are present, this vision pulls me out of depression, doubt, and despair.

For Noodlehead Marketing, our vision was Intentional companies reflecting excellence. We believed that marketing was a reflection of a company's foundational beliefs. This vision pulled us to live by example and to help companies discover their identity and reflect it in their marketing.

Here are other inspirational vision statements.

- *A computer on every desk in every home (90's Microsoft).*
- *A world without Alzheimer's disease (Alzheimer's Association).*
- *Creating churches that unchurched people love to attend (North Point Community Church).*
- *To offer designer eyewear at a revolutionary price, while leading the way for socially conscious businesses (Warby Parker).*
- *The world's most loved, most flown, and most profitable airline (Southwest Air).*

Without vision, we perish. We lose hope, and without hope, we have nothing to strive for or hold onto when life gets tough.

With vision, life becomes beautiful. We reap fruit we never knew possible. Through these difficulties, we discover the most meaningful achievements and rewards.

This is vision.

And Mission, is how we get there.

Mission Anatomy & The Four Pillars of Effective Business Strategy

You've got motivation and passion for doing something. You've got a picture of what it looks like when you've succeeded. So, how do you leverage that motivation to move towards the end goal?

You need a mission.

And the mission is our "how." It moves us forward. It's how we travel from the starting point to our finish line, and the potential pathways are numerous (*so we've got to pick one*).

How will you live out your purpose and arrive at your vision? What route will take you to the destination? Which one best leads you there?

When we travel to another city, there are multiple ways we can get there. Each route is a potential mission, and each has its strengths and weaknesses.

Business Mission Statements

A mission helps to unify and move forward, teams of people working towards a common goal. It gives a focal point to the here and now, to what's in front of us today.

For Noodlehead Marketing, our mission was **to obliterate marketing neglect.** Our team's active hunt was to find and eliminate the marketing gaps for our clients. Clients who aligned with this mission hired us to accomplish this strategic objective.

Get inspired by the following company mission statements.

- *Spread ideas (Ted).*
- *To create and promote great-tasting, healthy, organic beverages (Honest Tea).*
- *To create a better everyday life for the many people (IKEA).*
- *To accelerate the world's transition to sustainable energy (Tesla).*
- *To organize the world's information and make it universally accessible and useful (Google).*
- *To lead people into a growing relationship with Jesus Christ (North Point Community Church).*

A strong mission statement is an ongoing guiding force. It drives the many little things that happen daily and keeps us focused.

But, underlying these organizational missions, when the founder is involved, is the owner's mission.

The business has a driver. What mission is driving her?

Personal Mission Statements

A personal mission provides insight into how we'll move our life forward.

Not only are missions crucial for grounding and growing successful companies, but a founder's underlying personal mission is also the bedrock from which it builds. For the maximum success, we'll want to know how we align with our company and ensure our personal intentions are in harmony.

My personal mission, **to Share Life** with others, is propelled by my purpose and pulled by my vision.

My personal mission statement used to be *"to teach and inspire others,"* but I realized it was a one way street of me giving. I changed to its current iteration to capture my goal of both giving and receiving — a conduit of both.

Sharing life with others fuels my day-to-day priorities and actions. From my purpose, Jesus shares life with me, and my response is to empty myself of all He (*and others*) have given me. The more equipped I am to give, the more I receive. People matter and I elevate this value when it conflicts with business objectives.

Mission focuses us on the here and now. It guides us on what we can do today to get where we want to go tomorrow.

The Mission Formula: Strategy, Goals, & Actions

Like purpose and vision, the mission can also seem like an ethereal concept and one that's hard to nail down or understand. To help you box it in, let me share the three contributing elements making up effective missions: strategy, goals, and actions.

Let's explore the first; strategy.

1. Mission Contains Our Strategy

The strategy is a guiding force (*or series of them*) across our goals and actions. They're specific in direction, but general in specifics.

Is our strategy one of efficiency? The shortest and fastest route? Alternatively, is it the scenic route, one where we enjoy and appreciate the journey?

Strategy informs the underlying currents harmoniously moving pieces of our mission forward. Categorically, how will we execute our mission?

The answer to this question will illuminate our strategic direction.

The Four Pillars Of Evergreen Business Strategy

To succeed in our mission, we'll need to effectively use four strategic levers as we execute actions towards our goal.

How will we solve problems, differentiate (*position*), leverage, and promote our strengths to most effectively succeed at our mission?

Here is the definition of each.

1. **Offering Strategy:** What value do we provide (*in the form of products or services*) and what problems do they solve?
2. **Positioning Strategy:** Why must clients hire our organization (*as opposed to competitors*)?
3. **Leverage Strategy:** What advantages are we specifically able to extend for our customers (*because we're uniquely able to do so*)?
4. **Promotion Strategy:** How do we perpetually cultivate awareness and encourage reception of our offered value (*facilitate the decision to buy the offering from us*)?

Taking the time to clearly articulate what we offer, what differentiates us, how we're able to uniquely extend the differentiator and our approach to communicating this to the world will set you ahead of most small businesses that never answer these questions.

While they are hard problems to solve, answering them will set the stage for what will help us move the needle forward.

2. Mission Contains Our Goals

A goal is a defined area that dictates we've scored, moving us towards mission completion. A **SMART goal** is specific, measurable, achievable, relevant, and time-bound.

When our strategy is efficiency-oriented, our goal determines when we reach that efficiency and specifically defines how efficient.

When do we want to arrive at our destination? What are our checkpoints along the way? How do we know we are on track, and when do we know we are off track?

When we've completed one set of goals, it's time to identify the next. While many times we'll set goals to launch and create new things, our goals should steadily shift towards sustaining and improving initiatives already in place (*as to avoid unintentional abandonment*).

And, goals lead us to action.

3. Mission Contains Our Actions

These actions are the specific behavior we'll impose to change the state of things. They're directly tied to our goals, used to fulfill the strategy, and required for mission completion (*and ultimately vision*).

What individual steps will we take to act out our strategy and meet our goals? What habits and behaviors are turning the gears of our mission machine?

Without action, nothing we've talked about with mission, strategy, and goals matters. Action makes our intentions real. It's only theoretical if we don't apply these concepts to the real world.

With a good understanding of mission in place, let's dive into the details of mission using myself as a living example.

My Vocational Mission: *Moving Companies Forward. Together.*

My target client is a stalling e-commerce small business. Whether they're stuck, struggling, suffering, or striving, I seek founders wanting to get to the destination, but are unable. They need help, but they need more than a coach. They also need someone to help make stuff happen while strategically reoriented these activities towards a sustainable business model.

A contract co-founder.

My mission statement, **moving companies forward, together**, encapsulates this sentiment perfectly. Wherever they are, whatever they need, I'm here to augment in that way to help push the small business forward.

To get more specific, **I grow small business revenue, teams, and owners.** While the order and starting point may vary, it's these three levers that provide the short and long term gains required to sustain our engagement and ultimately foster the creation of a sustainable growing organization.

The Four Pillars Of My Effective Small Business Strategy

Within mission (*how you move your business forward, live out purpose, and trek towards the vision*) lies the strategic guidelines directing us forward.

Here they are again.

1. Offering Strategy. (*Our solution to the problem*)
2. Positioning Strategy. (*Our unique target audience Focus*)
3. Leverage Strategy. (*How we're uniquely tailored to deliver*)
4. Promotion Strategy. (*Our ongoing persuasion*)

As we explore these four facets of our mission strategy, it's helpful for me to first visualize them in a metaphor of changing a car tire.

In this visual, we've got a problem, a flat tire and need for a working one. We have a wrench (*offering*) to tighten the bolts and switch it out for the spare in our trunk.

When we use the wrench on the lug nuts, the position we choose determines if and how easy the process of loosening the bolts will be (*It's hard and involves knuckle injuries to do so when the wrench end is near the ground*).

If I'm loosening the bolt and I place a long pipe over the wrench, I'll have significantly more leverage to loosen the lug nut. What may be doable but hard with the wrench (*even with strong positioning*) is easy with the pipe (*leverage*). Positioning and leverage change the game.

The final of the four pillars is the promotional piece. How do we effectively communicate the problem we solve (*offering*), whom we solve it for (*positioning*), and how we're able to address that issue (*leverage*) uniquely?

The answers to these questions are what transform a small business from mediocre to top-tier.

And when you as a small business can answer these four questions, you'll be far ahead and tremendously more focused than any of your competitors.

Let's practically explore these four ingredients using my consulting practice as a living example.

Offering Strategy: What's The Solution You're Offering?

Business is about solving real-world problems. What's the solution your extending to the marketplace?

Here's how it unfolds for me.

What's critical for small business is cash. How much money is coming in, and what amount is going out?

When I begin a paid engagement with an entrepreneur, it's urgent (*in many cases*), we identify how we're going to move the needle in the right direction, quickly. Money buys us time to continue building sustainable systems. **Ultimately, I want to be in a position where an organization is foolish NOT to work with me because the provided value far exceeds the expense of working together.**

After growing income, building up teams is the second facet of my offering. The priority of growing teams is coaching and working one-on-one with leadership to help them develop into the leaders they must be for the organization to advance. Secondly, I'll work alongside the founder to launch and facilitate a talent development program to develop a cohesive culture and robust internal relationships. In other cases, I'll manage projects and work alongside this team to lead by example, and coach along the way. Thirdly, I'll work with small businesses to build virtual freelance teams that deliver what they need while providing financial flexibility.

In addition to growing revenue and building up teams, I'll work directly with the business founder to help extract, articulate, and communicate their vision. They need a guide to look at the business from an outside perspective and provide relevant insights (*especially the ones that are challenging to garner from the inside*). They also need help with concision, chopping down the large number of things they think they need to say or do, down to only the essentials.

However, it's ultimately up to them to establish direction and move everyone forward in unity.

Where cash is low, teams are lacking, and founders wandering, I come in and grow revenue, build up the people, and equip the small business owner. This describes my offering.

While my mission is to move the company forward, I'm here to help carry the burden for a time, not do it for them indefinitely. While there may be moments and seasons where this is necessary (*or messy*), the intent is that we both understand the goal, and we work together to accomplish it. Together, we build a sustainable system that outlasts my time as a paid consultant. Our engagement will eventually end, and how well we did will be graded by what happens when I'm gone.

To go deep and have a powerful influence requires this three-pronged approach. And, every small project we do together moves the organization closer to the end game.

Positioning Strategy: What's Unique About Your Client?

What's unique about the clients you choose? If you were to narrow this answer down, so there was only one client on the planet, how would you describe them?

Understanding our offering, and who is best positioned to benefit from us solving their problems requires multiple filters.

As part of this exploratory exercise, we're going to get so specific we eliminate all options. However, before we land on our final positioning, we can pull back from the single target so we can realistically build a small business around this audience.

So, what does my ideal client look like (*be thinking about yours as you read through the list*)?

- They are a small business owner, married, and with five or more children (*I'm one of the few that can relate*). Inherently (*via the owner's beliefs*) or explicitly (*the organization's purpose/vision*) our personal intentions (*purpose, vision, mission & values*) align.
- They've owned their small business for at least four years, and they have fewer than fifty employees. They lack alignment across teams and departments.
- Their small business has a substantial web presence with digital lead capturing, and online B2B transactions.
- Part or all of their team operates virtually. Most of their customer's interactions are virtual.
- They've failed to build a sustainable and steadily growing company. Annual revenue is stagnating or decreasing over the past two to four years. When they make systems, they fade away and are rebuilt later, again, and again.
- Their small business wants to use Hubspot or Joomla, but are leveraging outdated systems instead.
- Their marketing and sales efforts are both important. It's vital that they effectively work together. These efforts have failed to live up to the operation's level of excellence, or the operational excellence has been unable to deliver on the marketing promises.

- They operate as a technology or training e-commerce company.

Getting this specific has me slightly terrified, and it should do the same for you. I could even get even more specific. In some of these areas, like the first bullet, I'll need to settle for merely being a parent (*instead of having five children*).

Historically my positioning has narrowed as my consulting journey matures, and it will continue to do so. Get as specific as you can, and get somewhat uncomfortable, but understand this focus will develop over time (*and we can pull back if we go too far*).

And, here's a little secret about exclusion. As soon as we draw boundaries, everyone outside them quickly asks us if they can be the exception. Prospects outside this will come to you wanting to work with you, even when they are not your target. At that point, you have the option to either accept or decline their business.

Leverage Strategy: What's Unique About The Provider?

What's unique about you as a provider? What makes you a minority? Are you a monopoly of talent a prospect can't get anywhere else? And how does your uniqueness specifically compliment your target audience?

The answers to these questions will give us the leverage to more easily do hard things.

Using myself as an example, let's explore a list of features that I'm able to leverage while working with my clients.

- I'm a fifth generation business owner understanding, feeling, and experiencing all facets of entrepreneurship as the founder, coach, follower, friend, and family member. I've seen it all, and over my entire life.
- As a former small business owner, and current freelancer still operating a small business of one, I'm in the trenches of small business from different perspectives. I feel the pressures that come with the territory.
- I can operate in chaos (*where others would run*) with a movement towards sustainability, and breaking down complex issues in disruptive environments into bite sizable action items. And, I have a fair and flexible engagement and billing system to compliment.
- My Adaptability to lead strategically, follow tactically, and play the role needed to fill the gap, prevents your small business boat from sinking and propels us towards the end game. This ability also includes meeting people (*and their company*) where they are and moving us forward from that point.
- My technical aptitude, appreciation, and understanding include Hubspot, Joomla, Zapier, Airtable, & MailChimp.
- Marketing aptitude for writing compelling messaging, tactically executing SEO, and email marketing are additional vital skills.

- My intimate knowledge and experience with marketing, sales, and the relationship between them provide clarity and stamina for the process towards high performance.
- My in-depth experience with content marketing from the ground up and maximizing a bloated and stagnant content program gives me a full picture for effective growth campaigns relevant to current trends.
- My strong ability for developing talent and building a collective of self-starting learners, and teachers is useful for cultural improvement. Through my efforts, I'm developing lasting leaders, robust relationships, and cohesive cultures.
- I'm competent at extracting insights and helping people know what they think and believe. I'm steadily equipping them to act from this clarity.
- My experience and skill in making messages and stories concise and compelling are critical in a noisy marketplace.
- And I'm always listening and learning. From this activity, I'm seeking opportunities for improvement. I'm making things better and building sustainable systems beyond myself.

If chaos or over-committed are words commonly used to describe your small business, you must hire me as opposed to a technical freelancer, or a marketing firm because I'm uniquely able to jump into the chaotic trenches of your organization, get a foothold on where you are, and take baby steps to move us out of this state into a sustainable one.

When the metaphorical house (*your small business*) is burning down, I'm the one going into the flames when clients and team members are fleeing the scene (*in the most extreme examples*).

When we're working together, I'm communicating, sharing insights, and working under accountability. Sometimes I'll succeed while other times I'll stumble, but I'll teach along the way. The stakes are high for small businesses because errors are consequential.

For many freelancers, they can be unreliable, or if they are trustworthy, they may be highly technical oriented. What my clients need is someone who can handle tactical tasks, but also understand how each task plays into the larger picture.

When small businesses hire marketing companies, those organizations operate with set processes and have a hard time adapting to the needs of a small chaotic organization. A founder needs someone to jump into the trenches, meet them where they are, and help them move the business forward from that place.

When it comes to leverage, I'm able to press more effectively and with more force than others doing similar work. And you want the same for your business.

This leverage example is an intense look at what makes me unique and why specific clients should seriously consider working with me.

And this is leverage. With leverage, we have the opportunity to create, grow, and maximize it. If we lack in any area, we can shore it up, so our future efforts are more effective with less energy.

What, in your small business, uniquely gives you leverage to serve your target audience?

Promotion Strategy: How Will You Persuade Them To Buy?

With a robust offering, positioning, and leverage, we now must communicate these critical messages to those that would refer work our way, and most importantly to those we are expressly set up to serve. We benefit from a promotion strategy that informs how we'll go about persuading people to consider, explore, and eventually engage with our business.

In your small business, what current initiatives will you follow to grow the number of customers? Will you focus on new customer acquisition? Are you retaining existing customers more effectively? Will you leverage outbound or inbound marketing efforts? What about cold calling or networking?

Our articulated goals and our responses to the other three strategic pillar questions dictate our answers.

Let me provide an example by way of my consulting business.

One of the most important steps I took in starting this coaching business was deciding my target annual income and the number of hours I want to work each week (*you can explore this further in Path of the Freelancer*). As of writing this, my monthly target is 117 hours. Generally speaking, I need two to three clients allocating a majority of this time and a half-dozen others with a handful of hours each. With my small freelancing business, I only need a handful of clients to succeed at the highest level.

Because the work I do requires an intimate level of engagement with the founder, they must trust me to help them forward. This tension informs my three-pronged promotion strategy (*Relationship Maintenance, Building Authority, and Excellent Work*).

Relationship Maintenance. The three months preceding my shift from marketing small business owner to a freelance consultant, I met with about a dozen people per week. I reconnected with old friends and developed relationships with new acquaintances. So when I transitioned, I had a full plate of work within a month based on the cultivated relationships from this time, and the years before it.

And since then, I've continued to maintain various relationships without an agenda. People care about each other, and stronger relationships foster great value. At times, they may become a client, others may refer, and some may be good friends to discuss things and spend time together.

While relationships are great, being an expert is critical to our small business success. This reality is why I've leaned heavily into **building the authority of my expertise.**

In the three preceding months to this consulting journey, I began blogging and have done so consistently since January 2014. These blogs go out via email and social media, and much of the content is discussed and shared with people. Publishing books also contributes to this initiative.

My last strategic arm of persuading people to work with me is the proof of the things I say, put into action. **Excellent work** leads to my clients continuing to engage with me, and them referring prospects my way. These are the two easiest and most profitable sources of paid client work, and my approach here leverages them both thoroughly.

Often, others send skeptical business owners my way. Through our working relationship, that comes from growing their income, their teams, and themselves, they learn to trust again.

Moving On

With this guide and my example of its application, it's now up to you to work through the four pillars of a sound and strong business strategy. **Offering, Positioning, Leverage, & Promotion.**

When paired with a strong mission, clear goals, and an articulated strategy, your actions will individually and collectively move your business forward and upward.

Exploring core values is our last pit stop as we unpack the **Formula For Intentionality** and build a strong business foundation. To prevent us from veering off any cliffs, we need to make sure we have guardrails up. They "*protect and direct*"[17] our efforts.

---

[17] *Stanley, Andy. Guardrails, guardrails.org.*

Within What Guidelines (*Core Values*) Will You Operate?

Before we launch our business, we'll ideally want to draw two sets of boundaries — one personal and one for the company.

Not having these boundaries results in not having a beacon for when we go off track or when others take advantage of us. Core values equip us to draw these lines.

These values flow from within us. They are how we believe we, and others, ought to operate. They are what we determine as most important. They are a set of our core beliefs founded on what we have decided to be the highest priority truths.

Core values contain us and keep us from derailing. They help hold us together, and to see when we or others cross the boundaries. They dictate our duties and equip us to respond appropriately. They inform how we hold ourselves accountable when we cross over.

Here are my personal core values.

- Love of God, people, and self.
- Mindfulness.
- Openness.
- Accountability.

At Noodlehead Marketing, our core values were to

- ...actively pursue <u>excellence</u>.

- ...be accountable.
- ...be passionate.
- ...respect & serve others.
- ...actively change to become better.
- ...always share & listen to ideas.

Values constrain us, and in the short term, can feel like roadblocks to our success. But in the long run, values ensure the foundations we build in life and business last a lifetime.

My personal core values influence many aspects of the systems and ideas I implemented for my work. The same will be right for you as well.

Embrace The Formula For Intentionality

These sections wrap up our exploration of the formula for intentionality, and the elements you need to discover, define, and communicate your way to success.

Why?

Where?

How?

Within?

While you spend the time to work out these answers, I leave you with some practical insights for navigating the transition to this newfound clarity, particularly around the concept of vision.

How to Move Forward When Your Company Lacks Clear Vision

Those of us in the business world know what it's like to lead without a clear vision. It's challenging to lead a team or follow a leader when we don't exactly know where we're going.

It's in these moments we lean on fundamental business practices and strategies to move us forward, regardless of our vision. It's especially important to do so when we're in a context that requires wins to happen quickly.

As entrepreneurs, we're planning and building our businesses according to our vision. Imagine this construction project as a wall-building project. When we don't know what the wall (*or vision*) looks like or where to build it, it doesn't have to stop us from making bricks. Bricks are useful regardless of where we build and what type of wall we construct.

So in our business, what are the bricks (*strategies, projects, and actions*) that will be a part of your wall regardless of the type of wall you build?

Finding Your Vision

After shutting down my business in 2014, I wasn't sure what my next phase of work would entail, so it was difficult to know what I could do today that would be beneficial to the end goal.

I lacked a clear vision of my vocational future. Would I work for someone, start a new business, freelance, become a missionary, start a non-profit? I didn't know, but I didn't have the luxury of staying in uncertainty. I had to act because I had a lovely stay-at-home wife and four kids (*now five*) depending on me to provide.

Shutting down my company had become one of many projects and initiatives that when done, had me starting over from scratch, instead of each effort building upon the last. I was tired of starting over.

Here was my plan.

First, I would focus on cultivating **authentic relationships** with agenda-free meetings. Second, I would **communicate proactively** with my network, prospects, and clients. Third, I would **focus on the projects in front of me,** and the clients who were paying (*as opposed to neglecting their project while I sought out the next one*).

When you look at these three approaches, it's easy to see how they would contribute toward any direction I take in the future. They help me now, and they empower me later. **These efforts were all useful bricks to build (*as part of the metaphorical wall project*) even when I was unsure of my destination.**

This describes the practice of building bricks, knowing the bricks would someday be used to create a wall, towards a known vision.

It's ultimately about good stewardship in each moment. When we improve the people, culture, and systems around us, we'll position ourselves to more effectively execute the overall vision when it does finally arrive (*or we find it*).

And these regular activities over time are essential for making progress.

It's Time To Go From Visioneering To Achieving

On the horizon of possibilities, visionaries see all of the potential visions. This ambiguity is their Achilles heel. They see all the paths they can take, but they struggle on the choice of which one to choose. Starting everything (*with good intentions*), and finishing nothing is their hallmark.

They are chronic abandoners, with a wake of broken promises on their path. They seek to shape reality as opposed to accepting reality for what it is. And the great clash ensues.

The Visionary

But, it doesn't start this way. In fact, at the offset and much of the journey, being a visionary (*or a starter*) feels terrific. People look up to you, prospects want to work with you, and team members are loyal, even during challenging times.

As a visionary, you are the focal point and the receiver of admiration and attention. And it feels good to be the bottleneck forcing everyone to flow through you. As an inspirational guru, people are always looking to you for help solving their problems. Through this, visionaries find meaning and identity.

However, there's a dark secret for those of you who have been or are in this visionary state. You were courageous to leap from where you were to what could be out there, but you have little to no real idea on how to identify and land on the destination. You didn't think that far out before leaping (*and that's part of the problem*).

You don't know where you're going.

And, if you did (*or when you do*), you're hesitant to sidestep the spotlight for the destination (*vision*). By setting a vision, and telling people where it is and how to get there, you feel as if they won't need you anymore. You'll become replaceable, and that's scary.

It feels better to be the visionary than it does to extract that vision out of you for the benefit of the people you lead. And the process is no cakewalk, either. Doing this means being accountable and disciplined. As much as you might want to set a vision and get your team there, the price is higher than you're willing to pay.

The Cost Of A Visionless Visionary

But if you don't set your vision, you'll one day alienate and upset the people that love you most. Eventually, when they realize you're not *"all that and a box of chocolates,"* they'll see you for who you *really* are. A charismatic but incomplete leader. Someone who frantically changes by the winds of circumstances, and a leader with fatal flaws that makes their life harder than it needs to be.

You can step aside, cast the vision and direct your people, or you can perpetually disappoint them and eventually, they'll stop following you.

Level Up

Here's the good news. If you take this leap of faith, set the vision, and move forward together, you'll find a new and better role with your team and clients; An Achiever (*or finisher*) that consistently accomplishes great things. You won't just be the creative problem solver; you'll be somebody with merit-based authority that invariably makes a real difference in the lives of people.

Upon this newfound clarity, it won't be about you. It'll be about the vision. While loyalty (*or lack of it*) is still important to you, what's more important is how everyone is contributing towards the common goal. People will follow you because they know that by doing so, they will accomplish great things for themselves, their families, and their communities. And, they'll receive a deeper meaning in the challenge of pursuing this higher vision, as well as a reward for the discipline of actions required to make it come to life.

Reality Stands In Your Way

> *"Reality is that which, when you stop believing in it, doesn't go away."* - Philip K. Dick, *I Hope I Shall Arrive Soon*

To lead this way will require you to fully embrace failure (*an aspect of reality you're resistant to*), as part of the overall equation of business development. Choose to go from admiration to humiliation.

To set a vision requires a willingness to be perceived as foolish (*not everyone will like what we decide, or fully understand it*). And to be a fool for what you go after.

I learned that one of the most effective ways to memorize someone's name is by calling them the wrong one in front of a large group (*not always the best idea for fostering a good relationship*). Yeah, doing so quickly made a fool of me. But, I won't ever forget that person's name. This struggle is how achievement works and how the success and failure compound from it.

We take risks and sharply do things. When they work, we're ecstatic. When they don't, failure is carved deep into our mind and spirit. We learn, and we grow. What we succeed at is much greater than the suffering and embarrassment we face along the way. Often, it can even be an additional motivator to help us achieve in the future.

Accept reality. Learn to dance with it.

This marathon is no sprint. Our preparation for and actions during the extended journey must accurately reflect this reality to succeed. Do the hard work. Commit to a vision. And if it's wrong, you can always change it later.

Spend the time extracting your small business vision, commit to that focus, and lead your team with a strong sense of clarity and focus. Let your actions validate your intentions and finish everything you start. If you choose not to start a new thing until you've closed the loop on all the items on your plate, you'll begin to shift away from the long history of reckless abandonment and neglect.

Please start the process now, so when people who knew you five or ten years ago meet you in the future, they'll be in denial about how much you've changed for the better in ways they would never have expected.

Marketing Is A Reflection. What Are You Reflecting?

We've all heard the saying, *"Fake it until you make it."*

When my wife and I started the business, the phrase above would have been a good one to describe our company. Being great at marketing gave us an advantage of presenting ourselves as bigger and better than we were. We stretched and exaggerated our past and associated success to prop ourselves up with current prospects.

Before we launched the company, I worked with my uncle at his animation studio, and we were a part of an Emmy award-winning project. We also worked with various TV networks and prominent organizations while working together.

When we launched Noodlehead, we attached the Emmy and our high-caliber clients to our marketing efforts in hopes it would help us achieve our goals. In reality, it did the opposite.

When we present ourselves, it is important for us to deliver on the expectations we set. Because of our lack of experience and maturity, we were inconsistent in providing what we promised. We also alienated many potential great clients because we elevated ourselves so highly. Many prospective clients who wanted to work with us saw our pedigree and thought they could not afford us.

It's ironic how our efforts pushed away excellent, accommodating prospects while attracting customers we had no realistic way to deliver on their expectations.

As we progressed in our journey, and our company transformed, we began to ask ourselves, **what is marketing?** At the time of asking this probing question, we began to look at how marketing worked and the results it generated.

In marketing, we're attempting to communicate our message, and it's our way of expressing the value we bring to market. The value we offer comes from our experience and beliefs. Our beliefs come from who we are and how we see ourselves.

"*Marketing*" is a representation of who we are, and a reflection of the strong business foundation we create (*or neglect*). This external manifestation of our identity is how we communicate who we are to the world around us, and it goes further than a website, social media, and search engine rankings.

When "*Marketing*" is a representation of who we are, it causes us to accept that we cannot market well unless we know well who we are.

In our company's early years, we didn't know who we were, and it caused our company to re-discover its identity in 2011. From that point, we realized how important this was, and our company's vision shifted.

We started as a company helping fulfill marketing projects, and we changed to a company assisting other companies in discovering who they were. Marketing became a result of our foundation building efforts.

When we use this definition of marketing, it surfaces a gap for us. The difference was our "*fake it until you make it*" attitude. When marketing is a facade and not an accurate reflection, this marketing definition holds us accountable. It probes us to ask ourselves why we are not presenting ourselves authentically.

In our business, we began to see everything we did externally as marketing; a reflection of who we were. From how we presented our office, to how we communicated in emails, it was all evidence that we were what we said we were.

Our team, clients, and friends saw the good, the bad and the ugly. Our reflection was one we strove to portray as accurate as we could even when we did not like how it looked.

When we did not like what we saw, we chose to change instead of hiding, and it was these drivers that helped transform us from an outside-in marketing company to an inside-out marketing company.

The same could be true for you.

Are you ready to step out into the light?

8. Step Three - Lead Your Dedicated Team Forward

As we're transitioning from chaos to order, and from wandering to grasping a focused vision, we'll want and need the team we have to come along with us.

Unfortunately, it doesn't usually work out that nicely. Some folks will come along while others will depart. In other cases, we may have to fire people who should leave but instead choose to hold on to the bitter end. Other times, we may lose people we thought were essential to our organization.

This part can get messy. However it plays out, it's critical we focus on bringing our team along (*both existing and new*) and equipping them to lead with us. The before and after transition team share our history and will help successfully fulfill our vision.

To build a robust, scalable company is to build up people. Without this, we might as well stay small or go freelance.

Start thinking about the company employees as your customers. If we ask them how well you're serving them in the ways they need it, how would you score?

Mentoring Is At The Heart Of Entrepreneurship

As business owners, we're teaching our team the vision and how we're to take care of our customers. With our company leadership staff, we're showing how to guide their respective functions of the business. The capacity of our company comes from our team's collective ability to lead. The best way to increase this capacity is to level up our organization's leaders (*as you level up yourself*).

So how do we best go about this?

Teaching.

Let's discover this by understanding the four levels of teaching, how it applies to business, and we'll then explore a framework for action.

The Four Stages of Teaching

The first of the four phases is when we are the student, taught by the teacher. We listen, and we ask questions.

Once we've gained an understanding, we become a practitioner. Practitioners have learned and realized the nuances taught to us, and they apply them in real-world applications. These real-world scenarios surface challenges that force us to adapt our perspective and foster a deeper understanding of the underlying principles we've practiced applying. We'll eventually gain experience, leading to a pearl of more profound wisdom as to how it all fits together. Over time, we master our craft.

Our third stage is teaching students and practitioners. This stage is our opportunity to fill the gaps in what we know, and more importantly, to understand how we know what we know. Our students reflect our strengths and weaknesses, and they act as a real-time mirror. Current practitioners (*our former stage*) challenge us with how the principles and fundamentals help them in the real world.

The fourth and final stage in mastering our craft is teaching teachers. It's the step that ensures the insights we leave behind will live on beyond us, and it fuels a culture that builds a scalable well-functioning business.

In this stage of teaching, we are two steps removed from the student, and our diluted level of control illuminates additional challenges and growth opportunities as we learn the final gaps in our understanding. This stage is both the most challenging and rewarding.

The Stages Applied To Business

These four mentoring stages also reflect the progress of a small business. Before fully launching my company, I acted like I knew what I was doing, but deep inside, I was scared and unsure of how to make it happen. As a student, I tapped into teachers around me, both good and terrible ones. While learning from these teachers, I was also delaying the actual jump into full-time entrepreneurship.

It wasn't until I got a push from my wife to either launch the business or get a job that I leaped from student entrepreneur to a practitioner. I quickly realized the limitations of my head knowledge as real business challenges came at me from multiple directions. How do I find new clients? How do I deliver on the work I've sold? How do I hire people to support me? How do I manage all of these dynamics all at once? Chaos descended upon me, and even amidst certain levels of success, the business, stress, and anxiety overwhelmingly followed.

My lack of maturity (*and missing courage*) as a business owner hindered my ability to address these questions effectively, and I struggled through the process. However, I learned and grew as I cultivated a team around me.

As I got a handle (*after many years*) on what I was doing and was able to make progress, I shifted into teaching my leadership team. How could I equip them to lead the company without my constant hands-on involvement? This moment is when I showed my team while simultaneously tapping into resources and programs for effectively handling their respective functions of the company.

As they got a good handle on their respective role in the business, the challenge I faced shifted to them teaching those that followed their lead within their functions of the company.

This shift also changed what my leadership team needed from me. How could I teach a level of ownership? As a small business owner, it's much easier to go past my leadership team and deal directly to make things happen, but doing so can be short-sighted and relationship breaking.

These downsides make it challenging to build a scalable business. The key is to embrace these challenges and changes to grow our company. If we do, we can set a plan for anticipating and moving to and through these stages.

Take Action On Mentoring Others In The Business

Flourishing, as a small business owner, requires we share what we've mastered. Sharing what we master is about teaching what we know and sharing stories of success *and failure*.

In our journey toward success, we'll pass **four mile-markers** indicating we're moving in the right direction. These four checkpoints help us step through the four stages of teaching in our life and business.

The first checkpoint is when we are seeking others out to share our insights and stories. Others share their current business challenges, and we feel an immediate connection. Impulsively, we share how we overcame in similar situations. After sharing with multiple people, we'll realize how much our insight helps, but we'll also face the challenge of our limitations. We only have so much time to share one-on-one what we know.

Out of this limitation, we'll pass our second mile-marker where we **broadcast what we know**. Through short-form writing or public speaking, we'll begin communicating our insights publicly with others so more people can benefit than those we have time to meet with individually.

As we continue to share with others in this capacity, we'll realize the limitation of our insights. While it will help many, it fails to address the intricacies and nuance of each's circumstances.

It's at this point where we'll need to **dive deep into the lives of others in ongoing mentorship**. At the same time, we still have the limitation of time, so we'll leverage **group mentoring** so we can go deep and wide. This place of actively mentoring others is our third milestone in our journey to share what we've mastered.

As we progress down this road of teaching, we'll soon realize that we won't always be available or even alive to help others. So, how do we help people beyond our capacity or lifetime? How do we leave a legacy that will impact generations to come?

It's at this point where we seriously explore **a permanent beyond-us system** that helps many more when we're unable, unwilling, or not around. Here we write a book, create video courses, record audio podcasts and tap into multiple mediums to capture what we know in a way others can explore when it's appropriate and relevant to them.

With a mindset of creating a beyond-you system, you capture the mindset of creating a scalable and profitable business model.

The scary challenge is recognizing your lifetime contribution to the business and preparing yourself to willing let your company go.

It's not until we learn to release willingly, that we'll consistently experience growth. Proactively letting go allows us to embrace the journey of progress.

To recruit and grow a team in quantity and quality, requires the guiding force of mentoring. But, regardless of how well we might do this, we will need to subtract certain team members while also adding others.

Navigating The Addition & Subtraction Of Team Members

There's no way around the complex challenges of recruiting, managing, and terminating team members.

With enough experience, we'll face both growth and decline in our small business journey.

However we go about it, it's critical we're deliberate and realistic with the process as to prevent and minimize terminations, and extend the longevity of aligned team members. I haven't always been.

How A Zealous Hiring And Ongoing Avoidance Accrued Debt and Kicked A Bad Decision Can Forward

> *"Just as the rich rule the poor, so the borrower is servant to the lender." - A Hebrew Proverb*

Debt. It brings up a range of opinions, feedback, and feelings. My father expended an abundance of energy, teaching me the dangers of debt, urging me to steer far away from it. In some ways, I heeded his advice. What I didn't realize was how many indirect roads there were to this debt.

After starting Noodlehead Marketing, committed to operating debt-free, I still found myself in debt on three occasions, and they were the result of bad decision making, not merely the process of borrowing money to go make something happen.

In late 2008, I needed a salesperson, or at least I convinced myself I did. I was not going to change my mind. It was just a matter of finding someone to fill the role, and I received a recommendation from someone I admired. Because hiring this person was going to give me what I wanted, and I was inexperienced (*it was my first salesperson hired*), I ignored several flags and jumped into a flawed arrangement.

After three months, this staff member was not generating the results needed to sustain his participation on the team. However, he was switching industries, going from selling products to services, and we didn't have a sales system in place. It was chaotic, and we even worked out of our condo (*no office*). Everything was going against him to start with, so unless he knew his stuff coming in, there was no realistic way for him to be successful.

I also struggled to hold him accountable because I felt like I needed him. My fear was, if I held him accountable, he might leave. **It's funny (*but mostly sad*) how our fear-induced actions guarantee what we fear will come true.** After three months, we ran out of money to pay him. At this point, I should have cut the cord and let him go, but I was too attached and committed.

I needed it to work. We just needed more time. Underlying all this, was my struggle to acknowledge my mistake. Instead of facing this harsh reality, I chose to avoid it and to push it to the future.

Debt tends to be a symptom of avoidance. Instead of waiting or addressing the issues we need to discuss, we instead choose to procrastinate. Borrowing money enables us to avoid the problem and push it off into the future.

So instead of cutting it off with this salesperson, we continued for three more months hoping things would turn around, and he would collect enough income to pay for himself. It wasn't enough time, and ten thousand dollars of credit card debt later, I was forced to make the change I heavily resisted.

Instead of letting him go, I prolonged our agony and changed his compensation to commission only. It was the easiest way for me to let him go (*instead of doing the hard thing of firing him*). Eventually, he found another job, and we formerly parted ways.

My problem was not the lack of a salesperson, it was that I learned about the idea of hiring a salesperson, and I attached myself to this shiny object. It was my silver bullet to success, and I was going to get what I wanted. When I got it, I was not willing to let it go, even when it hurt the company (*and my family*). We maintained a destructive cycle to me, the salesperson, and the company.

When we ran out of money, and we had to go into debt to continue, we should have decided to lean in and deal with the reality at hand, before it got much worse.

The key here is preventing this scenario from playing out. While I learned a lesson, it wasn't enough to prevent more hiring problems from arising. My elusive white whale was hiring a reliable and successful salesperson.

How To Wisely Approach Hiring High-Impact Leaders

> *"Test everything... Hold on to what is good." - Paul, an Apostle of Jesus*

While hiring a high performing salesperson didn't work out in the previous story, things changed. Connecting to another sales representative led to me getting distracted once again.

The stars aligned for my little business to land another successful sales representative on a commission-only basis. And just like that, I got what I wanted. Unfortunately, what I thought I was getting was not what I received.

While this team member embodied many strengths where I as a leader was weak, their attitude and lack of alignment to the company vision was hugely problematic. The situation got to the point where I had to fire this team member, not based on merit, but on a continuous toxic attitude that negatively affected the team and me.

Before I got to this point, I did every possible thing I could think of to help this rep, but my investment was in vain (*at least it felt that way*). A year later than I should have, I finally pulled the trigger and fired this person. It was emotionally devastating for us both.

Like my first sales rep hire, there were flags and issues, but I chose to ignore them. As a result, I had to deal with the issues I invited into my company, and in the end, it cost me time and money (*both things I was short on*).

So, how does a business owner go about hiring and not end up in this type of situation?

With research and testing over an extended period, we can prevent most of our staff troubles.

Hire slowly and deliberately.

On the research side of recruiting, talk with former team members who've worked with them. How was it like working together? How much did the person direct, contribute, or guide? Many times a successful project is driven by someone behind the scenes, not always the one taking credit.

On the testing side of things, explore smaller endeavors before handing them the reigns entirely. Please get to know them, and what it's like working together.

After I shut down my company, I didn't expect I'd become a full-time freelancer. With several of the companies I explored working with initially, I proposed that we start the process by doing some contract projects. This approach would provide value to the company, let me earn income, and give us both a chance to explore working together.

If it made sense, we could progress the relationship. If it didn't, we could go separate directions. I find it foolish that small businesses don't explore this contract option before hiring more often.

We must realize that not everything is as it seems, and we need to do our due diligence to find suitable partners to prevent hardships on relationships and succeed on large projects. Sometimes when we do this, it may involve tactics that are contrary to the culture we're working within.

When the Only Good Option Forward is Parting Ways

When it comes to firing an employee, I lean towards doing whatever it takes to make it work. But doing everything possible to reconcile and move forward is not always fruitful. It's in these moments where the unpleasant decision to fire someone is required. And if there was one thing I liked least about operating a business, it was firing people.

One difficult employee situation resulted in a year working to make it right only to end up pulling the trigger. In that case, it was a year too long. The stress of the situation made me sick, and the lack of the decision put a pause on moving the business forward.

In a later situation, where the relationship was quickly deteriorating, I moved swiftly to terminate the person, and it was still traumatizing for both of us.

When we work with people, we have relationships with them, and we also hold the responsibility of their family's provision. It's no small thing and one which requires deliberation.

I'm now more inclined to take care of people during the process. If pride, money, or other factors involved in my decision are present, I let these things go while also acting reasonably generous (*because I've hurt people doing it the other way*).

A third instance involved an independent sales contractor. He was also heavily resistant to authority and my direction as he pursues his agenda. I ended up restructuring his compensation to be driven by his activity (*instead of a fixed fee scopeless engagement*).

Unfortunately, this didn't change his approach, and he continued working on projects he cared about in ways he wanted to approach them. While that work was useful, it wasn't what we needed or what I requested (*in detail and writing*). Metaphorically speaking, he was trimming the hedges when I asked him to mow the lawn.

With the new structure in place, I reminded him multiple times along the way what would happen if he didn't "*mow the lawn.*" And again, I was specific and wrote it down.

Unfortunately, he chose not to do it and was extremely surprised when I followed through on my commitment to terminate the contract for how he responded.

While he didn't like it, I could empathize. He was in the midst of a financial crisis, and I was his last lifeline.

While the business didn't pay him, I did go out and buy a gift card with my personal money and give it to him as a gift. I wanted to let him know I cared about him as a person even though I had an issue with his production and conduct. He was responsible for his previous poor financial decision making, and I couldn't make bad business decisions because of his.

Very rarely does a firing end well, so it's our role to be deliberate about when and how we do it. We also need to make sure we do what we can to preserve the relationship and not let things or money make it worse. In firings, sometimes there is no right decision. It's merely a matter of choosing the best of two bad options.

With experience, we can anticipate this, allowing us to prepare and proactively address it. Doing so could create compelling opportunities for us to do something transformative in the lives of our team members.

Many of the issues small businesses have with turnover are the result of how they work together. Getting simple communication and accountability systems in place makes all the difference in the world.

How to Effectively Lead & Work With Our Team

The worst-case scenario is hiring numerous people and establishing a culture of chaos with each of these individuals. This approach pulls (*or stalls*) the company in a variety of directions, many unwanted. I've experienced the difference between over a dozen folks wandering in circles and a small group of four focused and harmonious people moving in the same direction. The latter was, by far, more effective.

To get the type of traction we want requires solid clarity with our team and the roles we each play.

Let me ask you five questions about how you interact with your team.

> **Key Questions**
>
> - Is clarity on roles consistently elusive?
> - Do you wonder who is responsible for different activities in your organization?
> - Is there an absurd amount of people in email threads and meetings as a result of role confusion?
> - Do you step on the toes of others to get stuff done amid this chaos?
> - Do you end up doing what someone else should be doing because of this tangled mess?

There are more questions I could ask, but you get the point.

I've led and participated with teams that are defined by this type of confusion. The exciting part of this problem is that the solution is quite simple. Define and assign the roles of each area (*Department, Campaigns, & Projects*).

The following metaphor helps us quickly establish the desired clarity.

Clarity On Roles And Responsibilities

Imagine driving an SUV from Atlanta, Georgia to Nashville, Tennessee. In this vehicle are four people.

Sarah is driving; Joey is sitting in the front passenger seat (*Shotgun*) helping Sam and Ellen, who are passengers in the back seat. We've also got backpacks, a cooler of drinks, and a few tools loaded up in the trunk of the vehicle. Now, while Sarah is driving the car, she doesn't own the automobile.

The owner of the SUV is Jack, but Jack is good friends with Sarah, who has proven herself to be a responsible driver. He's allowing her to drive it. As the owner of the vehicle, Jack is ultimately responsible for what happens to the people and the vehicle. **He's the one who decides who drives and rides in his car.**

As the driver of the vehicle, Sarah is responsible for getting the passengers and cargo to their destination. **She moves everyone from Atlanta to Nashville.**

Joey, who is sitting shotgun in the car, is responsible for assisting the driver Sarah; however she needs it. This role also includes addressing any of the needs of the passengers in the back seat. **Joey is a support to the driver.**

Ideally, **Sam and Ellen are providing value** for their participation in this mission. Otherwise, why are they in the vehicle?

Sam is a mechanic, so he's been brought along because the car had trouble in the past and they may need someone to assist, should it break down. Ellen is a talented musician, and she is along for the ride to entertain the group with her beautiful music and voice.

Everyone plays a part on the trip.

Roles & Responsibilities For Moving Projects Forward

Think of the vehicle as your company, department, or the project you're driving from one place to another. Use the following recap outline from the metaphor to discover the answers.

- Mission = The route we take to accomplish our goal
- Owner = Decision maker, authority
- Driver = Moves everything forward
- Shotgun = Supports the driver
- Passengers = Support the mission
- Vehicle = The thing (*project, department, company*) we're using to accomplish our mission
- Cargo = Resources needed to complete the mission

With this metaphor in place, please take the following questions to your department, campaign, or project and answer them.

Key Questions

- What is our mission (*strategy, goals, & actions*)?
- What is our vehicle (*department, project, etc...*)?
- Who owns this? (*owner*)
- Who is moving it forward? (*driver*)
- Who is supporting the driver? (*shotgun*)
- Who else is supporting the mission? (*passengers*)
- What resources do we need to move the vehicle forward effectively? (*cargo*)

Define each one. In many cases, one person may fill multiple roles. In other cases, a position may intentionally go unfilled. But, it's better to know this upfront than not at all.

By defining these elements, you'll have clarity on whom to speak with, who needs to be accountable, and how to measure success when you're working on moving projects forward. Once you have clarity, you can shift towards how to align your efforts.

How Motivations Affect Our Efforts

Intentions (*or motivations*) are the currents that affect our behavior, and this is true whether we acknowledge them or not. When we fail to explore them, we often find ourselves in problematic working relationships, unmet expectations, and disappointing project results.

Instead of avoiding the discussion of intentions, let's better understand what they are and how they affect us. Mastering motivation discovery will lay a solid foundation for all new working relationships. Doing this in the hiring process with regular checkpoints is vital to sustaining unity over the long term.

As an example, I have a long-term (*~10 years*) aspiration for creating a financially sustainable writing career. This desire means that the amount of time with my consulting work will slowly diminish over the following decade. Building my personal platform and publishing will take over these newfound and accumulating hours.

As a result, I begin all engagements with the end in mind. My goal is for the owner to excel beyond me (*as opposed to a dependency on my abilities*). To steward well and leave them better off causes me to structure and organize the work we do while also building a team that effectively handles the responsibilities.

While working with one of my Hubspot clients, it's been apparent how his ambition is determining how we position the company to achieve his goals. We doubled revenue, and he could very easily sustain the volume of business we've cultivated without growing it further.

At the same time, we've created a robust business model that allows him to expand to other cities, states, and eventually, countries. So the question he needs to answer is, does he want to build a sizeable scalable company or does he want to sustain a small company? His personal intentions matter because they affect the business strategy.

By defining our intentions for ourselves, we can better communicate with others how our motivations will affect the work we do. When both parties have defined these elements, we quickly determine intentionality alignment (*or misalignment*).

This clarity allows us to understand how best to help each other in our respective journies.

Catch and Release or Catch and Keep? How Letting Go Can Bring Us Together

When it comes to fishing, I enjoy catching, relaxing, and spending time with others.

For those unfamiliar, fishing involves the use of hooked bait, so when the fish bites, they can't get away. Simple, and it works.

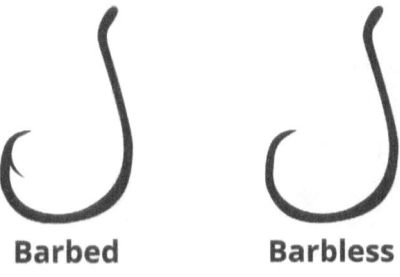

Barbed   **Barbless**

When it comes to hook types, there are two. The first is **barbed**, and the second type is **barbless**.

A barbed hook has a second hook that goes the opposite direction from the outward point. Once it goes into the fish's lip, it can't easily come out since the barb stops it. When we pull a barbed hook out of a fish, it usually damages it. If they've swallowed the hook, pulling it out can quickly kill the fish.

Fishing folks use this barbed type of hook when they want to make sure the fish cannot get away while reeling it in. They're usually used to **catch and keep**.

A barbless hook has no back hook preventing release. It pierces what it pokes, but it comes back out without much resistance or damage. When using a barbless hook, the fish are caught and released with minimal harm. The downside involves the fish getting away because when the line gets slack in it, the hook can fall out. Fishers often use barbless hooks to **catch and release.**

What does this have to do with business? Some systems and leaders catch and release, while others catch and keep.

Those who catch and keep, use barbed hooks. This approach is where they commonly create unhealthy environments (*the golden handcuffs*) and circumstances which would keep their employees from leaving in a situation where a separation is best for one or both parties.

On the flip side, there are team members who also practice this same behavior. They set up systems and circumstances which creates dependencies on themselves, and the deeper-rooted they become, the more difficult it is for either side to part ways, even when it is best for the relationship and individuals involved.

This behavioral pattern of creating dependency in either direction is like the practice of using barbed hooks in fishing.

Why do we choose this method? We want to survive, and anchoring ourselves deeper leads us to believe we are ensuring our survival. While It is understandable, it can also be damaging to the people involved.

Instead of creating a system of mutual dependence, what if we created systems which facilitated the independence of both parties? Imagine an experience where we both choose to stay in the relationship, instead of an unhealthy underlying motivation forcing us to stay together.

A relational ecosystem of catch and release is both empowering and terrifying at the same time.

Catch & Release Lived Out

Mutual independence of both parties is like catch and release. At Noodlehead Marketing, we believed this philosophy, and it manifested externally with our team.

It was most prominent when our leadership team went through a process to determine our company's purpose, vision, mission, and core values. We became intentional in our efforts, and we believed in surrounding ourselves with team members who shared our intentions.

After completing this process, we took the remainder of our team on the same journey. We all individually identified our personal and professional purpose, vision, mission, and core values. This process resulted in the departure of three team members.

One realized where she wanted to go in her life, and the efforts of Noodlehead Marketing were not taking her there. We became a distraction to her personal vision. When she realized it, we talked about it, and we came up with an exit plan to help launch her forward. We were sad to see her go, but at the same time, we believed it was also worth celebrating that she could move toward her dreams.

A similar situation played out with another team member where we helped launch him into his next career. He joined our team as an intern with the intent to switch from a non-technological industry into web development. Our company acted as a bridge to help him transition industries on his vocational journey.

When our time together finally concluded, we did what we could to help him achieve his goals and launch him forward. We made connections and sought marketplace job opportunities appropriate for his next step. Yeah, we helped one of our employees find another job even when this person was a vital part of our fulfillment team. **Our company was a launchpad.**

To serve each other in this way came from our intent to catch and release. **We don't own the people who work with us, so we should operate with a mentorship mindset when leading them.**

When we expect an inevitable end, it pushes for making the most of our time together and creating the most energy for parting ways on favorable terms.

Letting go of control, and trusting others in our relationships, is the type of connection which has a lasting impact on our lives and businesses, no matter how scary it might feel.

We always saw our organization as a springboard to what was next. When it was finally time for all of us to launch forward by shutting the company down, we had a great foundation from which to spring.

For those who intend to stay in business for the long run, the best team we can have is the team who chooses to stay because they are in alignment with values, timing, and vision. When that's no longer the case, it's time to figure out how best to help each other move forward. Ideally, we part ways with celebration and not a brutal divorce.

For Those Committed, How Will You Structure Your Work Environment?

Those leading a company will want to begin team relationships by understanding the terms of what it means to work together.

If we don't know how we'll communicate or hold each other accountable, we're setting ourselves up for disappointment and chaos.

And, micromanaging is not the answer.

Leverage A Visibility System That Includes Communication And Action Management

As a business owner, you want to control what happens, how it happens, and when it happens. Your livelihood and the success of so many individuals is dependent on a business reliably producing value for its customers, so it makes sense that you are hands-on with your business.

However, many small business owners take this too far when they remove their team's agency and dictate to employees exactly how to do their job (*instead of communicating their localized vision*). While they may feel and be justified in their doing so, micro-managing this way removes the mind of the team members and turns them into robots.

These team members become less effective at their jobs and don't develop into the leaders required to grow the organization. **While the owner gets the control they want, these founders end up disappointed, and their frustration leads to micro-managing even more, perpetuating the problem.**

The key for you to embrace is not focusing on solving problems but instead on **working to develop people that can solve problems without you.** And, to improve an accountability and communication system that equips you to teach and delegate appropriately. Fostering a safe place for your employees to fail in the short-term will empower them to succeed in the long-term.

If micromanaging is your go-to method, I encourage you to dig into the root of why you operate this way and discover a better plan for how you could more effectively grow your team (*and resolve your insecurities*).

Effectively And Steadily Move Your Team's Actions Forward While Facilitating Their Leadership Development

I'm most successful when I'm looking ahead, defining what I want to happen in the future, and acting on this today.

Daily, weekly, monthly, quarterly, and annually is the target cadence for this. This activity forces me to stop for a moment, think about what I want, and articulate it. Doing so makes it more likely I'll make it happen and inoculates me from the pressure and criticism of others.

> *"Follow Effective Action With Quiet Reflection. From The Quiet Reflection will come even more effective action." - Peter Drucker*

On the other side, I (*and you*) grow the most when I'm reflecting and learning from the challenges and contradictions faced along the way. Journaling facilitates this. What have I done? What worked and what didn't? How can I change for the better?

The challenge with most of us is not the lack of ability to do these two things, but the lack of time, or more accurately put, the lack of prioritizing this time.

This tension is why my small business owner clients hire me. They want to force the issue and spend the time to do the thing they know needs doing but struggle to prioritize. While I can serve them for a season to build this habit, real success is when they continue without my involvement.

Leveraging Writing To Make This Happen

I've baked this looking forward and reflecting back, into my blogging schedule. The beginning of 2018, I laid out my goals for the year, and when the end of the year hit, I looked back at those goals and other developments. It was as an opportunity to memorialize the lessons and moments that came before it.

Throughout 2018, I continued this practice monthly, looking back and learning, and looking forward and planning. By committing blogs at the beginning of every month and year, it pushes me forward and provides another layer of accountability.

Looking forward and reflecting on the past are two fundamental habits for developing as a leader and accomplishing our goals. And these two fundamental concepts are the framework I'd use to lead and manage my hypothetical company's team. While you may not publish them in a blog, doing it privately in a journal or note-taking system will accomplish many of the same benefits.

How Learning To Delegate & Submit Transforms Our Businesses

Proactive scheduled communication and organized mutually visible actions are how you'll build a system that provides what's needed to grow the business while also empowering your team (*instead of crushing them with incessant hovering*).

As the owner of an organization, we are ultimately responsible for how our organization conducts itself. And, as an organization grows, it requires us to recruit and delegate authority as the workload increases.

Dave Ramsey uses a rope as a visual to convey the concept of delegation.[18] In the analogy, the cord represents responsibility. When it comes to trusting others with this responsibility, he suggests we hand someone the end of the rope and feed it to them until all we have left is the other end of it.

As a business owner, I went through a season where I threw ropes at my team and walked away, usually without communicating expectations. If I came back, and they had not done what I thought they should do, I was disappointed. Repeatedly doing this caused me to overcorrect, and it became a catalyst for another season of failure.

In this other season, I gave my team members rope but failed to feed them more responsibility. I struggled to trust.

Along the Noodlehead Marketing business journey, I learned to delegate, direct, and lead a team to our defined success. Once we understood the hazards of leadership and delegation, we decided to get specific when it came to delegating authority.

---

[18] Ramsey, Dave. EntreLeadership: 20 Years of Practical Business Wisdom From The Trenches. Howard Books, 2011.

Through an exercise which led to the restructuring of our company, we decided each department would have two leadership roles.

The first role was what we called the department *"authority,"* and the other was the department *"driver"* (*from the driving metaphor earlier*). The driver was responsible for moving the department, its people, projects, and actions forward. Department authorities (*the vehicle owner from the metaphor*) were responsible for decision-making and ensuring the driver was fulfilling their responsibility.

Each department had these two roles, and two different people could fill it, or the same person could wear both hats. We then determined five departments to which we would assign these two roles. One of the departments we identified was *Planning*, which was responsible for planning projects (*obviously*) for our clients. Good at project planning, I was the driver in this department.

We also identified the authority of this department. One of our team members, according to Strengthsfinder, was an activator so we believed it would be good to have her as an authority on this department. Her talents would help trigger our plans into action.

As the owner, I was submitting part of myself to the authority of another team member. And, it fostered a business structure of mutual submission within the company.

Delegation Failures

This new-found trust and clarity led to us seeing past issues we hadn't fully realized were happening. As we continued working with companies to become purpose-driven and vision focused, we saw these same issues with role confusion. These problems fundamentally fell into two categories. **Authority Abandonment** and **Override**.

We'd watch authority figures in other organizations chronically quash the driver's decisions if they executed it differently than the way they would have done it.

Imagine for a moment you are driving your friend's car. He owns it, but he is letting you drive. He is sitting in the passenger's seat, and as you are driving down the freeway, he grabs the wheel and attempts to take control of the car. In the struggle, the car veers off the road and into a tree. **CRASH!**

In business, this happens all the time. Driver override leads to timid driving. Timid driving leads to mediocre results. If every time we take the wheel back from those who are driving for us, they start to question their decision-making, and they become less willing to take risks. They begin thinking about what their authority would do instead of what is best for getting us towards our destination (*vision*); **'Why be creative if every time I take a risk, you'll override me?'**

Now imagine another scenario, the owner of the car gives the keys to his ten-year-old son. He's not taught him anything about driving, and he tells him to go to the store. If he can start the car, this scenario ends up in a crash. Hopefully, the kid's incompetence leads to a minor accident and not a horrific one leading to the death of people.

In organizations, this scenario happens often. When authority figures delegate without instruction or direction to those unprepared, they end up faltering. **The irony in these situations is that we tend to think it's the other person's fault, and we fail to see our neglect in the process.**

While there are appropriate times when we need to override or abandon, I believe it is best to minimize these situations and to make sure when we do it; we are doing it intentionally (*and rarely*). **Just because we have the authority to do something doesn't always mean we should.**

When we learn to define our roles, it teaches us how to submit to each other. When we learn how to submit to each other, we realize how much chaos we created when we were operating without clarity. With newfound visibility, we now quickly and easily see how the hazards of delegation affect us all. This revelation acts as a catalyst for change.

So, where are you on this journey? What is your next step in understanding the authority you have and the authority you delegate?

From Vision, Set Nested Goals During Proactive Planning

A key to effective delegation, as Ramsey states it, is to hand them the end of the rope and slowly feed it to them until you, as the leader, are only holding onto the end.

If I imagine launching a new business, here's how this practically plays out. With a new hypothetical company's intentions (*purpose, vision, values, & mission*) articulated, my first hire or contractor and I would have a clear picture of where we're going as an organization.

Nested under these intentions, we'd start the year by proclaiming our respective goals (*looking ahead*) and which of them we'd each be responsible for making happen.

What do we want to accomplish by this period's end that also aligns with the annual goals and the organization's intentions?

This answer clarifies and provides accountability as we share (*yep, it's two ways*). By doing this aspirational planning regularly, it makes daily and weekly goal time spent much shorter.

Not spending this time usually leads to a bottled-up reaction, and often an unpleasant one.

It also allows us to skip these checkpoints when the context requires it. **But, like brushing our teeth**[19], **the**

---

[19] Sinek, Simon. The Infinite Game: How to Lead in the 21st Century. https://www.youtube.com/watch?v=3vX2iVlJMFQ

key is consistency over time, which makes up for occasional misses along the way.

Lessons Learned From Past Experiences

At the end of each period (*daily, weekly, monthly, annually*), reflect on your goals and how successful or not you were. And, explore the lessons you learned along the way.

How do we change in the next sequence? How do we more effectively get stuff done and lead others (*or ourselves*)? This regularly scheduled reflection time allows us to proliferate, share what we've learned (*practice teaching*) and more quickly moves us towards what we've deemed as a success.

Communication Checkpoint Cadence Expansion With A Growing Team

Whether it's a quick morning chat, weekly meeting, or a monthly email digest, establish a minimum level communication cadence. When we miss a checkpoint, we have a trigger to follow up with them. This activity will actively bring you along on what's happening and alleviate your anxiety from the unknown.

It also provides an opportunity to capture ideas and share direction. Usually, this cadence will start often and dwindle in frequency as you effectively teach, direct, and empower your team.

As the team grows, I'd localize these day start and end sessions to relevant groups of team members. Eventually, weeklies would follow, and so on. The goal is never to eliminate these habits but to do them in at a pace that is most effective and relevant to participants.

Fading Will Happen, Fight It

> *"...we saw the continuous-improvement culture begin to erode when physicians leading daily "huddles" — short team meetings aimed at managing quality and safety — were busy with other duties or left the primary care practice."* - Aravind Chandrasekaran and John S. Toussaint[20]

As useful as this practice is, it's also hard to maintain. The research quoted above indicates the moment we begin to stop leading these regular huddles is the moment when the business begins to decay.

Many times in various seasons, I've failed miserably. But, the great thing about the system is if I flop today I have the opportunity to restart and get on track tomorrow. The ongoing tension also moves me forward, even when I'm not following it fully.

There will always be a tension to move away from this structure, especially when things are going well. However, when things are wrong, or there is too much going on, these cadences bring us back to the fundamentals we need for long-term success.

---

[20] Chandrasekaran, Aravind, and Toussaint, John S. "Creating a Culture of Continuous Improvement." Harvard Business Review (*May 24th, 2019*).
hbr.org/2019/05/creating-a-culture-of-continuous-improvement

As Business Owners, We Impact Many Lives: Let It Be For The Better

When we start our business and relentlessly pursue a goal, we entrepreneurs miss how many of our authoritative actions negatively impact those around us. Moreover, we usually fail to recognize the wake we leave behind (*many small business owners have never been an employee lacking the experience that follows*).

The wounds I inflicted on others is what I most regret from my time leading at Noodlehead Marketing.

It's an important lesson learned because of how it drives me to interact and lead people today. Unfortunately, this lesson took me some time to recognize and overcome. To truly solidify it meant reconciling with those I hurt.

My Wake Of Broken Relationships

In the second half of the Noodlehead Marketing journey, I made a list of everyone who worked with the company as an employee, contractor, or vendor. As I reviewed the record, it quickly became apparent how many people were on this list. As a small marketing business operating for only a handful of years, there were too many people.

As I looked through the list, several people popped out as instances where I failed and hurt them either through neglect or intentional action. In other cases, I was also hurt by them while working together. This pain also extended to several clients.

With a complete list of people on my reconciliation train, I now knew who I needed to forgive, and those whom I needed forgiveness. With others on the list, I was unsure of where we stood, so I connected with them to discover if there was some way we needed to reconcile. Was there something I did or said that hurt them, and I'm unaware of it?

The Train of Reconciliation & A New Approach

So, I began the journey of processing through over two dozen broken (*or potentially broken*) relationships, and my responsibility of where it went wrong, and where I was hurt. I let go of my resentment and forgave them as God did for me.

I began meeting with those who deserved my apology and my request for forgiveness. Some embraced this with open arms quickly forgiving and rejuvenating the relationship. Others told me to pound sand and never talk to them again. In one case, it took a friend several years of meeting to forgive me.

Ultimately, facing these people directly about what had happened, and owning my responsibility was transformational for our relationship, and myself as a person and leader.

I needed to express, to those who played a part in my life and success, my uncommunicated gratitude. In some cases, I wrote letters while in others, I met with them to share how thankful I was for their role in my journey. I could not have done it alone, and I wanted those who made an impact to know it.

Now, I live a life of real-time reconciliation. If I hurt you now, I resolve it promptly. If you hurt me now, I forgive you now (*and if appropriate, hold you accountable*). If you do something that requires gratitude, I express it immediately. There's zero tolerance for me to accrue relational brokenness or unexpressed thankfulness that I would someday address in the future.

I choose to live a life where I'm in good standing each day before my fellow man, and before God.

An Inspirational Story Of Reconciliation

At the turn of history, there was a despised and dishonest Jew named Zacchaeus whom Jesus shared a meal. Surprised, the surrounding community could not believe Jesus would meet with this terrible corrupt tax collector (*the worst of the worst at that time*). Jesus met with him, regardless.

After Jesus accepted and showed love towards him, Zacchaeus declared his dedication to the poor and those he cheated along the path to his financial success. He even committed to paying back four times the amount he cheated anyone. It's a profound story I've grown up with all my life. So while my failure or path of reconciliation was not as dramatic as this inspirational figure, it's one I can relate to through my journey of reconciliation with others.

Lead For The Better

For all the people we've led and the people who will help us forward, it's vital we understand how critical each person is to the success of the mission. And, to appreciate how essential it is that we steward these relationships with the level of respect and honor they deserve. **Our success at the cost of other people is never worth it, and it only leaves us with regret.**

Move your business forward with an appreciation for others, and desire to lead and involve them the way Jesus did so for Zacchaeus, and the way you'd want them to do so with you.

9. Step Four - Elevate Your Business With Bullet-Proof Systems & Mental Models

Without systems, your company is entirely reliant on your people, their abilities, and experience. If you've got great people, it's less concerning, but still costly. If they ever leave, you're in trouble.

It's also unfair to place the success and failure of the business directly on the shoulders of those moving the mission forward. A sustainable approach that minimizes burning out great people and taps into robust systems that function beyond any Individual.

A powerful way to test our existing systems involves a high caliber weapon, well at least for the mental exercise.

The Magnum Test: Will Your Company Survive Beyond You?

While driving to work, you realize you're running low on gas. You pull over to the next station to fuel up. While filling up your tank, you notice a poor lady getting mugged. You're the only one who sees this man holding a large magnum (*handgun*) at the lady.

Quickly, you lunge at him smashing his body into the wall and knocking him out. His gun drops from his hand and BANG! It fires as it crashes to the ground. You look down at your stomach and realize you're bleeding profusely. Sirens and lights dance around you as your vision fades to darkness.

And now, you (*the business owner*) are dead.

Your company must continue to deliver for the clients, and provide for you and your team's families. How well do they succeed without you? How much direction, systems, and a structure was in your head instead of documented and culturally ingrained? Does your company continue flourishing when you're no longer around?

What about if a key employee leaves? What happens to the people reliant on the success of this business? And their families?

If you can't answer these questions with confidence, you're likely lacking two solid ingredients for establishing active systems: a business blueprint, and a system architect.

Having these two pieces is the first step. The more important one is creating a culture of architects who can build and interpret these blueprints for ongoing success.

What Is A Business Architect?

A business (*or system*) architect is not only someone who can envision the result, but it's also someone who can direct the mapping of how to build this end goal into a usable blueprint (*a living business plan*). They're skilled at planning, but they don't stop there. They also understand what it takes to make it happen and bring it to life.

On its own, a blueprint is limited. Someone could hand us a plan to build a skyscraper in Atlanta, but that doesn't mean we could make the structure. And this is the difference between people and architects. Architects know how to create a plan, gather the team, execute the project, and do it in a way that lasts. They also teach others to do the same.

In a sense, good business architecting is like great parenting preparing kids for the future. An architect knows how to foster success and minimize failure. They understand what contributes to success, and they hold an appreciation for the people and systems that have come before them.

When receiving advice or hiring, beware of counterfeit architects who rely on a single success to validate their abilities. **The true test of an effective architect (*a founder, staff member, or contractor*) is one who can consistently replicate success in different and challenging scenarios.**

What Is The Business Blueprint & How Does It Work?

The blueprint is a single place where anyone could see how to operate any part of your business. It's ideally a living dashboard that allows anyone to see how a business is structured, who is responsible for these areas, and it also includes written direction. A blueprint should have enough information to operate each aspect of the organization without speaking to anyone.

A great example of this is the United States government. We have a blueprint with the declaration of independence, the constitution, and amendments. We've got the three branches of government and people are elected through a designated process to fill these roles. And hundreds of years later, these documents continue to guide us.

Different roles in the government facilitate the interpretation, application, and change to these blueprints.

A blueprint is also the DNA of your organization (*which may include an org chart but also goes beyond it*). Instead of it operating out of people's heads, a well-documented blueprint is as simple as possible.

As the CEO of your company, is there a place you can go to view the company blueprint and understand how it's structured and who is responsible for different areas, projects, and tasks? Can your team quickly get up to speed on the direction of the company by merely reviewing this dashboard? In my experience, the answer to this is usually *"not really."*

For my former marketing company, this was part of the shift that moved us from reactionary to proactive. We started with a spreadsheet and built the Noodlehead Marketing Blueprint. The clarity was catalyzing. We knew precisely how to move projects, and ultimately the company, forward. The connections between all the disparate pieces were now visible.

As a result of our internal success, we began helping our clients build blueprints for their marketing departments. They too experienced the benefit of this intentionality.

Unfortunately, while we realized we were equipped to construct these documented DNA portals, our clients were not. In many cases, they hired us to maintain them, which was disappointing for those of us who wanted to teach and free other business owners from their chaotic operations.

The most depressing example came as a result of one of our largest clients parting ways with us. With this transition, we'd now have a terrific example of this process playing out, or so we thought.

We had worked with them for over a year organizing their marketing department and projects. We were knocking out action items and getting stuff done in tandem with their team. We were also teaching their team how this all worked and guiding them through the process. However, when we finally parted ways, they hired someone new to oversee the marketing department, and it became apparent very quickly; this person was not interested in our system, or any organizational structure. He operated out of his head, and in a reactionary way.

After the hand-off, the incredible organizational blueprint work went into decay and disappeared without the owner's or manager's commitment. We handed this department off to someone who was not an architect and who had no interest in becoming one.

System Building Is Hard, So Where Do We Go From Here?

So the good news is I've got job security knowing I can consistently do something that provides tremendous value, but so few others are willing and able to accomplish. But, regardless of how difficult this can be, I'm partnering with my clients to operate this better way, even if it takes several years to pass it along.

When working with my customers, I'm looking to accomplish two things for them.

First, I provide a consistent quality example of what it looks like to construct a blueprint from scratch and sustain it over time. I seek to reveal the fruit of this endeavor. If in cases where a business owner can't or won't do this, they'll at least get to experience it firsthand. This example is their inspirational step required to value and embrace the practice.

My second goal is spending my time with clients and their teams to train them as architects. By asking questions, pointing out blind spots, and encouraging through inspiring examples, I'm slowly moving them towards an ongoing and sustainable way of building their project, department, and company.

While I fill a void during my time working with the client, my long-lasting agenda is for them to thrive without me.

A great and highly utilized architect is someone who systematizes what they touch and regularly hands these systems over to others for maintenance. It's a scalable and organic way to grow a business.

Where Do You Go From Here?

First, you need to adopt a framework to house everything. IDEMA is my preferred structure for business blueprints (*if you don't resonate with it, find an alternative project management system*).

Then, set up a spreadsheet or software tool like Airtable around this framework and begin capturing and organizing how you run your company.

As part of this process, you'll want to establish intentions (*purpose, vision, mission, and values*) for your company by defining the areas of your business and determining who is responsible for making actions happen. Under these areas, you'll want to organize projects similarly.

Ultimately, you'll want to create a blueprint that you'll use and review regularly. Housing your action lists in the same place makes this more realistic. Start simple and document the most critical items first. As you get a better understanding of how you run your organization, you can increase the blueprint's complexity.

The blueprint should house the things that allow you to know how your company runs. Make this your top priority until it happens. Moreover, don't let your team and their families be caught dead without it.

Bulletproof your business today.

The Persistent Weight of Reality & The Fight For Sustainability

In the classic movie The Terminator[21], a cyborg from the future is sent back in time to kill Sarah Connor, the mother of resistance leader John Connor. The entire film is her running and escaping execution by this relentless and powerful killer. With the help of a soldier from the future and some luck, she finally (*after being persistently hunted*) destroys the terminator (*with mechanical help*).

This story is an excellent overlay of what it feels like to survive in the challenging universe we live inside. This impending doom of striving to sustain our business

---

[21] The Terminator. Dir. James Cameron. Perf. Linda Hamilton and Arnold Schwarzenegger. Orion Pictures. 1984.

ruthlessly chases us with few moments of relief along the way. Eventually, it wears us down, and we are forced to face it head-on as we strive to hold back the tide.

While she had the help of a hydraulic press, it was Sarah who ultimately destroyed the relentless machine, empowering her to be the strong woman we see in the Terminator sequel (*one of my favorite movies*).

The Challenge Of Survivalism

In entrepreneurship, I've witnessed (*with myself and others*) how we chase the next form of provision to survive. We feel hunted by the reality of our obligations. In many cases, fulfilling these obligations is just beyond our reach.

From project to project, I witnessed a friend just barely getting by over the course of several years starting with when we first met. Several years later, he wanted help. He needed money to resolve the immediate situation in front of him (*again*). Seeing the pattern and wanting to solve the problem permanently, I offered to help him find a sustainable way to generate cash, to address the cause of his situation, not just the symptoms. He declined.

During Noodlehead Marketing, this played out for my team and me as we robbed Peter to pay Paul. A client recognized this pattern in their failed project and decided to cut ties. While unfortunate, it gave us a jolt and the practical financial margin to launch us forward with a better paradigm.

Most of us have faced this challenge and felt this weight in some form. But, it's accepting this reality and deciding to change the way we play the game that matters most. To do so requires we prepare appropriately so that we can move towards a better way.

Moving Towards Sustainability

The first step in facing this reality is diving deep inside to find out what we're truly seeking. Do we want help towards sustainability? Or, do we want someone to do it for us?

It's nice to have help. It's a blessing to receive from others, but if we're able, we must contribute towards wise working and sustainable management. Look in the mirror and commit to change for the better.

A legend goes that cows run the same direction as storm clouds while buffalo turn around and run against the direction of the moving clouds. Both creatures get rained and stormed on, but because the buffalo move in the opposite course of the clouds they minimize their time in the storm. Cows, running with the clouds, extend the negative experience.

If we turn and face challenges head-on, we'll reduce the amount of time and energy we give to the various issues that come our way. Doing so will lead to a more prosperous life for ourselves, family, business, and community.

Will You Create & Abandon or Build To Sustain?

In my experience as a business owner, and working with other entrepreneurs, it's quite rare for sustaining to take priority. Usually, visionary owners want to create and move onto the next thing without a second thought (*I know, I've been there*). Some will even abandon their business as they explore some shiny object with mixed results (*based on who is left behind*).

Unfortunately, this leads to the wreckage of broken and abandoned ideas. In these situations, the only things getting maintained are projects team members care for or those of which clients complain.

The Cost of Unintentionally Abandoning Our Creation

The cost of inadvertently abandoning varies based on the scope and length of time we've neglected an idea.

I remember when Noodlehead Marketing came across the shiny object of Bluetooth proximity marketing devices. We spent several months packaging, promoting, and selling them. We even had a meeting with a Fortune 500 company about these devices.

Unfortunately, the technology was not far enough along and had more problems than advantages. We weren't able to get enough traction to justify the ongoing effort, so we intentionally abandoned it to refocus on our primary business offering.

After refocusing, I quickly realized how bad of an idea this distraction had become. We severely neglected our main pipeline of building websites and helping market companies. Now the bills were coming in (*the terminator was on his way*) and we had to ramp things up quickly to catch up with the business.

But this wasn't the only shiny object I chased or thing that bored me. During the first several years of owning my marketing company, we were serially creating projects. I had multiple websites, landing pages, social channels, and even a YouTube video series called Pasta Salad (*about internet marketing tools*).

There were also internal wikis, project management systems, and CRMs. In many cases, we would launch a project abandon it, forget, and then do it all over again without memory of our previous effort. **If only we had sustained the first time around, we would have made strides of progress!**

Somewhere along the way, I decided to make a list of everything going on in the company, active or abandoned (*as part of the blueprint mentioned earlier*). As several hundred items accumulated on this list, for a small company of fewer than ten people, I saw my pattern of creating and abandoning, and it wasn't fruitful. I seriously struggled to finish and sustain. The result was a littered path of people, projects, and ideas. All that time, money, and relational equity squandered. We were fast, but our approach prevented us from ever building momentum.

Visionaries create and move on. Very few spend the time creating to sustain.

When we treat what we build like we would an actual garden, we can easily see the parallel of creating to sustain. Knowing what we create, as a living thing, helps remind us how we need to care for people like we do with these plants using sunlight, water, and soil. To foster flourishing our efforts can never stop.

Like this garden, our ideas, projects, and processes need attention and resources to continue. The success we desire requires less energy but more focus and discipline. At the core of it, struggling with these two realities (*discipline and focus*) is much of what drives us away from the mundane act of maintenance.

Three Real Examples To Further Illuminate The Necessity Of Maintenance Systems

How does this play out in work? Below are three examples to help inspire ideas for grabbing onto the mindset of planning to sustain and the systems to do so.

1 - How Website Maintenance Neglect Leads To Big Problems

For four years as a freelancer, and seven owning a marketing company, I've project-managed and built Joomla websites. In the year following my work, dozens of my client's websites were hacked as a result of them not upgrading their CMS software. In many cases, they didn't actively run backups, so it made restoration challenging (*or in some cases impossible*).

In addition to security, website content ages over time, and links change (*leading to broken ones*). While these two items are not the only elements that lead to a website decaying, the point is that the responsibility of creating a website spans beyond merely building and launching it. We must dedicate time and resources to keep it current.

I've got a client who built their custom online ERP system over the last decade. During the course of that time, the number of code lines has grown, but the development staff has not. At some point, the team will no longer have the capacity to build new projects. They'll work entirely on addressing bugs and keeping core functionality running. By the time this happens, it'll be tough to expand the team or launch new projects.

Ideally, a decision-maker understands what's required to sustain before they begin the construction (*as opposed to when the project is far along or completed*).

2 - Blogging With An Asset Mindset (*It's Not Trash*)

If there's one thing worth creating serially without looking back, it's an ongoing blog. While it will eventually decay and break, it'll provide significant benefits along the way.

I'm working with a client who had a noteworthy blog archive of almost eight-hundred articles. This effort was a vital asset for driving large volumes of organic traffic to his website. Unfortunately, much of the content decayed, becoming outdated with broken links. In other cases, there were multiple articles on the same topic ripe for consolidation.

The same is also true of my blog. I've often updated my services page, and I'm aware of how much my about page needs an update. Every blog I publish is also subject to future updates. As part of my writing and blogging process, I have a system for capturing improvement ideas for each blog, so when I revisit them, I can quickly implement the changes.

There are also broken links across my archives that require my attention, as well as other items on my maintenance todo list. While I have limited capacity to maintain, I do slowly and surely work through the items to move forward.

As my blog grows, so will the amount of time it requires to keep it excellent. Streamlining my processes is one way to address this, but at some point, I'll need to dedicate more time or hire help to steward it well.

3 - Staying Active As A Freelancer When Things Are Good

Freelancing is not easy, and merely focusing on the paid project in front of us is not enough to make the path work. When it comes to maintaining my freelancing career, I identified eight achievements required to do this well (*the framework for my first book, Path of the Freelancer*). For quick reference, here's the list.

1. Fully Committed To Freelance

2. Offerings In A Compelling Package
3. Steady Stream Of Paying Clients
4. Maximize Active Clients
5. Escape The Roller Coaster
6. Wise & Precise Financial Management
7. Unified Personal and Work Lives
8. Share What We've Mastered

When freelancers share challenges they're facing, I quickly identify which of the above achievements they're failing to sustain (*and so can you!*).

Even with the steady success, I've sustained as a freelancer; I need to stay active outside my paying clients. This action includes doing less urgent activities essential to long-term flourishing.

Blogging allows me to promote myself while also sharing what I've mastered as a significant way to help others. To minimize the emotional weight of feast and famine, I work with customers in an ongoing capacity, build a financial reserve, and engage with a meaningful community.

Preventing Chronic Abandonment Means Asking Key Questions

As perpetrators and victims of not planning to sustain, we at Noodlehead Marketing faced the consequences, and this driving factor was why we incorporated the idea of including maintenance planning during the discovery phase in the IDEMA framework.

By simply asking ourselves, what resources it'll take to keep the idea alive, we'll get a pulse check of what that entails. Entrepreneurs usually minimize the ongoing cost and effort, while operational folks will exaggerate the effects. A balance of the two while leveraging data provides a realistic picture of what to expect.

Here are four maintenance questions to ask when planning your next project.

> **Key Questions**
>
> - What actions will be required to maintain this idea? How often will they need to be done?
> - Who will make decisions on the project's maintenance?
> - Who will be responsible for moving the maintenance actions forward?
> - By maintaining this, what can they no longer do?

Plan & Execute With The Intention To Sustain What You Create

Whether it is our business, parenting, our marriage, the team's health, the house, or cars, maintenance is vital to thriving together. When we make decisions, especially the big ones, it's critical to the long-term success that we understand and commit to the entire iceberg (*not just the tip*).

This effort requires we plan and execute with visibility on what's expected to sustain. By knowing and experiencing the cost and benefits of doing it this way, it'll be hard to do it any other way. The IDEMA framework is a powerful way to systemize this mindset into your organization.

Three Principles For Moving The Needle The Right Way

The marriage between reality and making sure we create a sustainable system, and one that builds a profitable result, is vital.

Many creative entrepreneurs have tons of ideas, but they've lost sight as to how it will help the business move forward and make a profit.

It's best to figure this out before starting, so you can embrace the campaign for the long run. Remember, no one method is a silver bullet to solve all your growth challenges.

Three of Jim Collins principles for success[22] are powerful filters for our plan forward.

1. **Fanatical Discipline** - For us to succeed in our business, we must know our twenty-mile march

---

[22] Collins, Jim. Great by Choice: Uncertainty, Chaos, and Luck--Why Some Thrive Despite Them All. HarperBusiness, 2011.

(*the thing we do no matter what*) and ruthlessly execute it every day (*or week*) like clockwork.
2. **Empirical Creativity** - While creativity in business is useful, we must also back it up by its utility. Do our company projects generate a fruitful result, or are they simply creative with no practical benefit?
3. **Productive Paranoia** - We all worry things will turn against us in the worst moment. Productive paranoia expects, plans, and acts on this tension.

The second principle ensures we don't launch bad creative ideas. The first ensures we follow through on the good ones. The third transforms our fear into productive action (*We'll explore two of these in the following section*).

Do It, No Matter What

The following is helpful, but, If there is one thing you must do to make the jump, it's sticking with it.

Follow through no matter what. Pick something, commit, and no matter the obstacles or distractions, follow through. See what matters most as a bone you won't release.

Successful entrepreneurship is grounded and sustained. Anything else is simply a series of unfortunate events.

Additional Mental Models To Use & Share With Your Team

"The hardest part of the journey to personalized success isn't adopting the new mindset...it's letting go of the old one." - Todd Rose, Dark Horse

While external systems are vital to business success, there are also mindsets (*mental models*) we must embrace and live out for effectively bulletproofing our business. Without mental systems, an external one will fade away over time.

These additional models we'll explore in the following sections are not an exhaustive list, but a targeted one. These are the ones with high impact in helping you make the jump.

Before we dive into the details of each, here's a quick list of what we'll explore.

1. **Iceberg Effect:** There is more to it than you realize.
2. **Blind Spot Ownership:** We don't know what we don't know, so we need others to share with us.
3. **Proactive vs. Reactive:** Long-term matters most.
4. **Twenty-Mile March:** Doing what matters, no matter what.
5. **Pitch Free Operation:** Cut out speculative performance.

6. **Productive Paranoia:** Leverage worry as a productivity starting point, not a paralyzing state of being.
7. **Navigate Road Hazards:** What's worth a hard stop when challenges arise?
8. **Care About The 20 Percent:** The difference between surviving and thriving.

Let's jump into the first.

Mental Model #1: How The Iceberg Effect Illuminates How Much We Don't Know

> "...our human instincts, shaped for (and craving) a simple world, fundamentally mislead us in a complex, unpredictable world." - Jennifer Garvey Berger

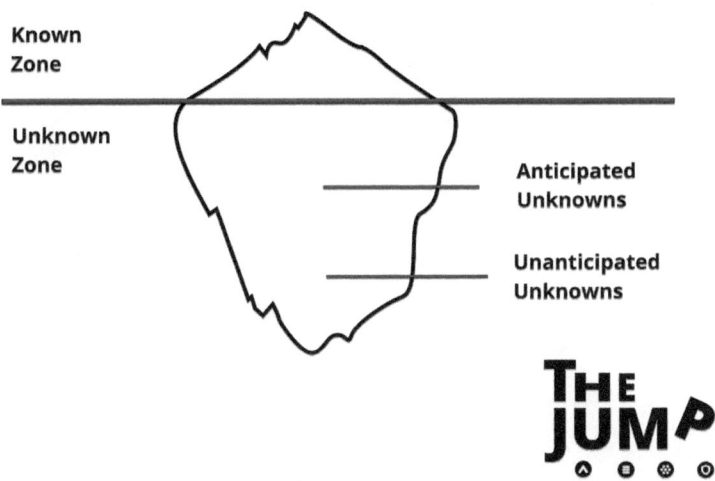

The Iceberg effect is a visual metaphor for realistically facing our work. When we face a project, relationship, employee, or client, the top of the iceberg is what we immediately see. Sometimes, it's the only thing we want to see.

When exploring a solution to our problem, we only see the tip of the iceberg (*something this optimist still struggles with*). We may think it'll only take two weeks to complete when in reality it's a two-month-long project.

Experience and discussion allow us to go deeper with our understanding. But, even without these insights, the simple act of mapping out everything we think is required to make it happen, and asking others for feedback, will get us much further along than most of us appreciate.

When we do have experience in a particular area, we visualize what the iceberg looks below the tip. We're grafting this experience onto what we see in front of us so we can make wise assessments. While we don't know for sure, we can reasonably anticipate the unknowns that are likely and unlikely to happen. This perspective helps us better predict the successes and failures we'll face along the way.

But, no matter how experienced and knowledgeable we are, we will inevitably face unexpected unknowns in life, work, and projects. It's a deep abyss with no end.

In 2001, numerous New York companies planned for what they knew and what they expected could happen to mitigate their risk and maximize their chances of success. However, no one expected a group of terrorists to attack the world trade towers and change the paradigm of their business, New York City, and Americans nationwide.

It is wise for us to plan for what we know, what we anticipate, and a little extra for the complete unknown. But there will always be a gap, and consequences we can't entirely prevent or overcome.

When the unexpected does come our way, how we respond is critical to overcoming and sustaining success along the way.

And speaking of blind spots...

Mental Model #2: Blind Spot Ownership - Why It's Important To Embrace That You Don't Know What You Don't Know

> *"It is the sick person who really knows what health is." - Oswald Chambers*

We all have blind spots. They're usually the things that we don't know we don't know and we'd be wise to seek them out proactively. But, for much of our young lives, we live in constant denial, thinking we know everything. *"No blind spots here!"*... We say.

However, expecting we know it all, or know enough that our lack of knowledge never causes us to stumble, is simply a slow-ticking time bomb for the moment when **we truly realize we don't know anything at all.**

The Liability of Not Knowing

It wasn't until after I was eighteen years old (*2004*) that I first flew on an airplane (*and on my own*). I assumed (*wrongly*) that plane boarding was on the other side of the security checkpoint. And I don't mean the corridor that leads to the plane boarding. I thought the plane would be boarded immediately after gaining security clearance. Completely naive, I didn't know, and I didn't even know to ask. No one ever told me.

As I now know, security is only the beginning of the plane boarding experience, not the end. Based on my unhelpful knowledge, I didn't get into the security line until shortly before my plane was about to take off.

Unfortunately, there was a rude awakening at the end of the security process when I came to realize that not only was my plane not there, but it was at the last gate in the corridor. It took me ten minutes to get there, and they closed the door when I was one-hundred feet out.

    "Noooo!"

I begged them to reopen the door and let me in, and thankfully they did (*Yeah, it was a miracle*).

My entire first plane ride (*to Atlanta, for my first time*) was me worrying about what would have happened if I missed the flight. Not knowing anything other than my fearful speculation, this anxiety-inducing exercise was not helpful.

Life, As A Big Unknown

This little story was symbolic of what was to come. Confident and ambitious, I thought I could take on the world moving across the country the following year in 2005. It was a year of many firsts.

- Getting married.
- Living away (*in house and city*) from my parents.
- Moving across the country.
- Transferring colleges.
- Experimenting with freelancing, online marketing, and movie making.
- Starting a business.

I thought I knew enough, but facing the brutality of real-life with numerous high stakes, quickly humbled (*crushed*) me, illuminating just how flawed, depraved, and inexperienced I was.

From the earlier wise words of Rocky Balboa, *"[the world] is a very mean and nasty place and I don't care how tough you are, it will beat you to your knees and keep you there permanently if you let it."*

Embracing Our Limits

> *"When we try to defend our egos rather than grow and change, we end up perfectly designed for a world that happened already, instead of growing better able to handle the world that is coming next."*
> *- Jennifer Garvey Berger*

My problem involved ignorance and inexperience, but arrogance played a significant role. I can handle anything, I thought. But, the moment we realize we can't, it's scary. Especially when we're isolated and trapped in survival mode.

While today, I've garnered volumes of experience, insight, and wisdom through my journey, I recognize there is still a deep chasm of unexpected unknowns out there I'm not aware of or prepared to face. It's not a paralyzing revelation, but a humbling one that drives me to seek the wisdom of God, the counsel of others, and the limited understanding of myself.

Responding To The Unexpected

Several years into our marketing company's journey, we decided to hire an office manager for the team. She was terrific for us. She embodied the strengths we lacked and was able to know what was going on and what we needed to address. I didn't always like her insights, but they were usually right on target. Her presence in the company made me and everyone better. Unfortunately, it was also a heavy burden and highly stressful for her.

So one day, she requested to meet with me privately and let me know she was quitting.

Wow!

This news was a gut punch, and all of a sudden, the burden she was carrying was now on me to move it forward. Without the maturity and experience I currently have, this was very challenging.

What I've learned from this and other similar scenarios is that we need sound systems where people play clearly defined roles. We also need to stay connected with a pulse check on our people, so we're aware of their involvement. And, we can't put too much on any one person because it's risky for the business and unfair to the individual. We should be regularly auditing each person with the magnum test. If they were to get shot (*with a gun*), what happens to the business?

Unexpected twists provide opportunities for growth. For me, I chose to grow as a leader and build a better company that was less reliant on one person. In other cases, it's been a catalyst to develop new systems and ways of working with people. Without these unexpected events, we'd miss out on these opportunities for discovering creative solutions to impossible problems.

Mental Model #3: Life & Water - Proactive or Reactive?

For years, we use a filtered water pitcher with two reservoirs. The top tank is where we added the water, and the bottom reservoir is where the filtered water was stored.

The top section only held a fraction of what the bottom could. To keep the bottom full, we filled up the top many times, but the filter's slow flow required a significant amount of time to fill the empty pitcher. The key was to fill it as we used it since there wasn't a way to accelerate the filter flow.

In our business, we can be reactive and attempt to fill our company's pitcher, but as much as we supply it, the filter can only process a certain amount of water at one time. If we're having problems in our business, reacting may be of help for a time, but there is limited bandwidth for it to take effect.

In sales, we can't expect our client relationships to maintain themselves. Over time, clients will feel empty, and they will start to wonder and question the partnership. The same is true for team members.

We can't resolve these challenges with a quick fix or a silver bullet. For long-term change and growth, it requires us adding water consistently to the pitcher and reaching out to these people steadily over time.

Reactivity says, fill it up only when it's empty. Reactive is a roller coaster of emotions and stress. Reactive never allows us to become full. Reactive is always a step behind.

Pro-activity says, fill up the pitcher every time we use it. Proactive is consistent and healthy. Proactive is always a step ahead and from a position of strength.

Like the pitcher, we also have limited bandwidth for giving and receiving. To live a life of thriving, this requires us to be proactive in maintaining what is important to us.

Where are you reactive? And proactive?

Mental Model #4: The Twenty Mile March Is What Your Business Needs To Move Forward

> *"Mediocrity is the sign of chronic inconsistency."* - Jim Collins

Jim Collins metaphorically struck me as I sat there listening to him in the middle of a Catalyst conference years ago. In his talk, Jim told the story of two adventurers in a race to the South pole. One of the two men made it there and back to base camp ahead of schedule while the other died along the way.

One of the three reasons (*the other two were productive paranoia and empirical creativity*) the first gentleman succeeded was due to his **fanatical discipline**. He not only knew what his mission was and the actions that went with it, but he also followed through on them. As part of the race to the South Pole, his response was to traverse twenty miles each day. Every day, no matter how hard the conditions were, he was going to log those twenty miles. If he was going to fall short, it was because nature wouldn't let him succeed.

On the flip side, the second man hoped to make it twenty miles each day, but he'd continually fall short and think to himself that he could make it up later. The next day, he'd have to knock out twenty miles plus the four he had to make up from the day before. Over time, he was running behind schedule doing what he could, to stay caught up.

When the opportunity arose, and the conditions were perfect, both of them were able to take advantage of the occasion, but only one was perfectly positioned to do so. It was the first man who was able to double his daily trek. The second guy was only able to go a handful more miles over the twenty.

Ultimately, the first man would finish the race ahead of schedule while the second would die before ever reaching the destination.

There is always going to be some obstacle making it harder than we hope, but the key is not how hard it is, but how we overcome in the face of these challenges.

In your work, do you know what your daily, weekly, and monthly marches are? Do you know what you need to do to make sure you keep making progress towards the end game?

If you can't quickly and clearly articulate the answers to these questions, it's time to sit down, reflect, and find the answers.

Mental Model #5: Pitch Free Work - Why We Ought To Leave Pitching In The Dust

Pitching is the idea of doing something for someone without their involvement and hoping it works out. It comes from a belief that our value comes from proving ourselves through excellent performance. We're worthless when we don't.

Examples abound from those who ask us to create. We go with little direction and our assumptions to develop what we believe the person will like most. We come back to the person with our *'presentation'* or *'performance,'* hoping the *'pitch'* will perform well and place us in good standing with them. **Those in need of this approval constantly are drained and never filled.** Pitching regularly ends with the surprise of rejection.

In many cases, we pitch because we fear conflict, facing reality, or being open. This fear drives us to isolate ourselves from whom we're working, instead of collaborating with them.

In business, pitching may look like our company being asked to build a project. We're asked to put together a proposal and presentation that will show them we can do something that will meet their objective. We likely won't get paid for our time, and they'll have several others competing for the business. Over the next week, we fight to win the work with no commitment from the company for our time and money spent. It's a connection on our part without loyalty on their part.

We hope to get the work, but often we're discarded for not meeting their uncommunicated expectations. At this point, we tend to become resentful. We worked hard, and it seemed as if they took our ideas and hired someone else.

For the times we win the business, we set the precedent that our ideas and contributions are of little or no value (*because we didn't charge for them*). From this point on in our engagement, we are more of a commodity, easily discarded when we are no longer of use.

Win or lose; it hurts. We feel used and abused. But we're responsible.

So, what are our alternatives to pitching?

Cut out speculative performance.

Lean into the relationship, foster an open dialog, and choose vulnerability. And, charging for not just the labor of doing, but the thinking that matters more.

Mental Model #6: Productive Paranoia - A Small Simple Practice For Preventing a Big Problem

Do you leave yourself margin should something go wrong? Do you strive for abundance knowing things will eventually make a turn for the worse?

Productive paranoia is the practice of doing something when you're worried something negative could happen. Here's what Jim Collins says.

> "10xers differ from their less successful comparisons in how they maintain hypervigilance in good times as well as bad. Even in calm, clear, positive conditions, 10xers constantly considered the possibility that events could turn against them at any moment. Indeed, they believe that conditions

> will absolutely, with 100 percent certainty-turn against them without warning, at some unpredictable point in time, at some highly inconvenient moment. And they'd better be prepared." - Jim Collins, Great By Choice

We can apply this in our business in both small and big ways. And its application could prevent significant troubles. While this fruitful practice is simple to implement, it can cause inconvenience or extra work. But, difficulty with the benefit of intentionality is an invited tension.

Here are ways I intentionally inconvenience myself.

Apply Productive Paranoia To Small Things

In 2015, I ordered my $1,300 high-end laptop. The reason I needed a computer was partially due to my son spilling a glass of water on my previous machine. Water and laptops don't work well together.

Now that I've got this expensive-to-replace computer, I behave differently around it when it comes to drinks. Usually, when I'm drinking my tea, I'll keep it in my sealed Contigo Autoseal mug. When I'm drinking from an open cup, I'll set it on a separate platform, table, chair so if it should spill it wouldn't spill over and ruin my computer.

Now when I'm at a coffee shop, I look around seeing numerous people with open drinks around their devices. All the potential spills! While people don't usually spill, it does happen, and I'd like to prevent that from ever happening to me.

Big Picture Application

While this productive paranoia mentality is powerful with small things, it also makes a massive difference with the big stuff.

As a freelancer, I've written a book about how to apply productive paranoia for freelance success. When work is good, it's only a matter of time before it isn't. When that happens, I want to ensure I'm as prepared as realistically possible.

For me, this results in actively paying down debt and increasing my financial margin. It also means I'm staying active on my blog, improving my services page, attending events, and meeting with people.

While I've had steady success for over a year, eventually circumstances will change, so it's best to prepare should it decline. If it doesn't take a downturn, I'll be in a stronger position to take advantage of opportunities.

When You Face Worries Don't Wait For Them To Get Better, Act-On Them Now

What actions could you take to alleviate your worries and fears? What could you do to prevent failure and maximize success?

Along the way, we'll come across worry and risk. Unfortunately, like facing a wild animal in real life, we'll likely freeze or panic responding in the absolute worst way.

Instead, it's best to accept the fear as a possibility and do something to prevent it, minimize it if it does happen, and have a plan to recover should that fateful day arrive. To do so requires deliberate planning and practice.

Mental Model #7: Road Hazards Of Life - Roadblocks & Potholes

While driving in any city, we come across potholes in the road, and they disrupt us when we hit them. We may spill our drink or drop something, and the movement is also hard on our vehicle and tires. While potholes jostle us as we travel, they don't stop us from moving forward.

POTHOLES are obstacles in our path we can drive through without having to resolve them.

When we are driving, there's another obstacle we face, the roadblock. It's an obstacle we can't overcome. In these cases, we must wait until the roadblock is removed or find another way to travel to our destination.

ROADBLOCKS are obstacles in our path we cannot drive through unless resolved.

So, how does this apply to our business?

Imagine we have written and scheduled a blog post for publishing in a few hours. It's not perfect yet, but we are willing to publish it. This tension would be a pothole. It's not ideal, but it won't keep us from going forward.

Imagine we are building a website for a client and we need the content for the site before we can move forward (*otherwise they'll have a beautiful website with blank pages*). In this scenario, getting the copy is a roadblock.

More seriously, imagine we're working on a marketing project. Our boss asks us, while planning out this project, to use a false testimonial for the project. For some of us, it may be something we are not willing to do, a roadblock. For others, they may not want to do it, but will. For them, this is a pothole.

As a believer in genuine marketing and being truthful, I advise against this approach. However, the point of the illustration is to illuminate the difference.

The next time you run into an obstacle, use this mental model to know how to navigate and communicate the challenge. Is it a pothole (*I don't like it, but I'll go forward*) or a roadblock (*I won't go ahead unless resolved*)?

Mental Model #8: The Eighty (80/20 Rule) Percent That Only Generates Twenty Percent Matters

It's commonly known that twenty percent of our client work leads to eighty percent of our revenue. Less leads to more results.

When we recognize this, we quickly lose sight of or dismiss the eighty percent of our clients that only generates twenty percent of our income because it's not worth our time *(seemingly)*. But this larger group providing a smaller percentage bridges the gap between surviving and thriving, and from good to great.

Whales eat thousands of pounds of krill, plankton, and other small life forms each day. This source of food is tiny and weighs almost nothing. It's only through eating vast numbers of these little creatures that whales get the intake they need to live and grow. The same is true with our earning potential.

Take, for example, my client workload from January of 2018. Three of my clients made up 95 of my 122.25 hours for that month. They were the twenty that earned me eighty percent. Seven other companies, the eighty that made up the additional 27.25 hours, generated 2,400 dollars.

Not tapping into both changes turns a $10.7k month into an $8.3k month. That's a big deal for me. As a freelancer or small business owner, $29k/year is no small sum. That extra amount allowed us to accelerate our debt, pay off our minivan, and in the future, make retirement savings strides.

The diversification of income across multiple clients also minimizes our financial risk. If we lost a client, we only lose a fraction of our income.

The key to long-term success requires the belief that every dollar matters. Because for every thousand dollars, is one thousand individual dollars. Each one makes a difference, and the many small amounts quickly add up to big ones.

Prioritize the twenty percent of clients that generate eighty percent of our income, but don't neglect the eighty that creates the rest.

Cultivate High Impact Systems & Mental Models In Your Culture

To exit the wandering stages you've found yourself stuck inside, will require an organized culture of improvement and focus.

You'll need this ecosystem to take advantage of your personal growth, the firm foundation you've built, and the loyal and remaining team dedicated to your vision.

So, what are the priorities of your organization, department, project? Who is responsible for them? And what are the activities happening in those areas by those people day-to-day and week-to-week?

If you don't have an answer, it's time to create the blueprint for housing the data you need to understand the answers to these questions. This clarity allows you to know that ideas, actions, and projects are being captured and given attention. It also allows you to check-in discreetly (*or explicitly*) on activity to ensure things are going as expected while not visibly hovering over your team.

> **Key Questions**
>
> - What framework are you using to organize ideas?
> - What tools are you using to manage these ideas?
> - How are you going to ensure that projects are completed correctly?

These seem like simple questions with simple answers, but many projects go awry when we don't define and clarify the answers to these questions upfront.

While working with customers on our targeted projects, I put on my SOFI (*Seeking Opportunities For Improvement*) goggles. Focused on the task in front of me, I'm searching for problems and challenges to overcome.

While this proactive mindset helps, you also need a way to capture and organize what you find. And this is where IDEMA, the framework for capturing and sustaining ideas, comes into play.

With a bucket for different types of ideas and projects, we have a way to organize and easily document them for future reference. With a framework, we leverage a project management tool for tracking ideas. This resource allows us to receive and give accountability on various tasks and projects as we have visibility of everything going on and who is involved. It becomes our map for moving projects forward and ensuring projects get done.

To help navigate the difficulties of managing a team, we'll want to understand each other's motivations and how they affect the work we do. We'll also want to establish a structure for how we'll engage and how we'll manage projects. This foundation will set the stage for success or failure.

Wrapping Up

Life and work are hard, but I think it's of utmost importance that we create well-designed systems to prevent the negative scenarios we see in the business sector.

Prevention is always the best solution, but when we find ourselves in these scenarios no matter how well we've planned and set up systems to prevent them, we need to work through them deliberately, communicate explicitly and ultimately ensure people are taken care of in the process.

This big and final step to making the jump is a powerful way to empower your team (*and yourself*). IDEMA could be the system you need to stop micromanaging your team, and rebuilding the trust you need to grow the business to the highest level.

Preferably, the company (*and you as the leader*) establishes a method for how you will all work together. Ideally, both you and your team embrace the structure and adjust it for maximization. It'll be necessary to make the most of this final step. And with it begins the transitional phase.

10. A Five-Phase Process For Transforming Your Messy Business Into A Well Oiled Machine

Companies, especially younger led ones, have a way of getting themselves all tangled up and unnecessarily complicated. I was a prolific culprit in my business building out systems for what they'd eventually become, not what they should be now (*yeah, I got ahead of myself*).

Overly complicated organizations also fail to plan out their endeavors properly. After years of business operations done this way, there's a big mess that needs untangling before the company can move forward and thrive (*Yep, that's me raising my hand again*).

Eventually, no matter how much potential for success is ahead, the business engine seizes and prevents the organization from moving forward. So the potential is lost because the organization is not able and trained to take advantage of it.

It doesn't have to be this way.

Ideally, a company follows a framework to accurately discover their intentions and foundations from their origin, using something like IDEMA. In reality, they rarely do. This deficiency describes my business ownership journey. It wasn't until the halfway point when things were chaotic and not working that I realized it was time to get intentional and decide what type of business I wanted to create. And how we'd get there.

But as hard as it can be in the moment, there is hope to make it out alive and build an agile and active small business.

The following personalized strategy is a way for tangled companies, departments, and teams to regroup, set a new stable foundation, and establish a pattern of healthy growth. And while the untangling process may be simple, it's the preceding steps we've taken through the book that will equip you to not only complete the process but stick with it, perpetually.

But, there's one critical concept to grasp before executing this strategy unless you like repeating the untangling process.

The Underlying IDEMA Framework

IDEMA (*Yep, I'm going to keep talking about this beautiful framework*).

The power of grasping the full picture of what we tackle comes through our exploration of the IDEMA framework. As visionary small business owners, we're prone to launch without a plan, without understanding what it takes to keep it going, and without an end game.

These exploration tendencies on their own are not a bad thing, but in the context of running a business, there's a new level of responsibility. **A company affects the lives of our family and all those connected to the business through the team and vendors, so we must take it seriously if we're to thrive long-term.**

On the flip side, no one wants to travel in circles perpetually. Defining and arriving at our destination is an exciting and powerful motivator. And when your ready, the following transitional strategy is designed to get you untangled.

Without an appropriate underlying system in place before transitioning, you'll get yourself all tangled up again. And that's where IDEMA comes into play.

Imagine that you have a way to capture and organize all ideas for improvement and problems to solve. Picture what it looks like when almost all of your projects are properly planned out. Think about finishing all those numerous projects you start only abandoning them when you've intentionally done so. Imagine everything created is stewarded with excellence in perpetuity until it's time to re-evaluate. And lastly, imagine a business that's continually reviewing and improving every aspect of itself as seamless as you breathe air.

You, as the founder and leader of your team, are fulfilled. Your team is satisfied and excited to be a part of the business and something greater than themselves. Alongside your fantastic team are lovely clients that make it a joy to continue serving them. And lastly, everyone is making money and receiving an abundance of value by being a part of your highly capable and healthy organization.

That's my vision for your small business. And IDEMA is the structure to ensure this happens, once we get through the transitional phase.

If this is what you want, and are willing to accept the responsibility for doing the hard things to make it happen, the transitional strategy will move you to the next stage of the process. And should you fall back, you'll at least be practiced at executing it the next time you get tangled up.

But before we review this specific five-step auditing process, let's talk about auditing.

The Power Of An Audit

Key Questions

- Are you doing something the way others have always done it? And, without testing or revisiting if it is the best way to approach the problem?
- Is there a better way to do what you were doing, but for whatever reason, your company has not switched to the better way?
- Have you ever wanted evidence the actions you were taking were having the desired impact?
- Do you suspect there are ongoing activities in your business that should have stopped long ago?

If you're asking yourself these questions, you now know the value of an audit. People, circumstances, and resources change, and we must continuously iterate to stay productive. Otherwise, we'll fossilize and go extinct (*just like those dinosaurs*). An audit *(stage 5 of IDEMA)* reassures and guides us forward.

It helps us to see what is working and affirm it. It helps us to see what needs improvement and change it. It helps us to see what is no longer working and stop it.

To gain the value of an audit, we must take ourselves through an uncomfortable rigorous process. For a moment, we feel exposed, but it's essential for growth and improvement.

The Three Layers Of An Organizational Audit

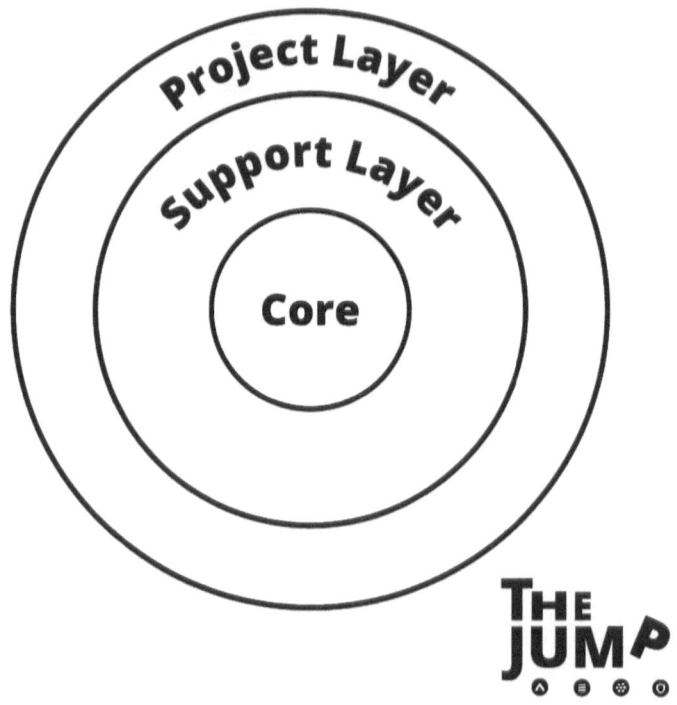

When running an audit, there are three areas we focus on this effort. This audit includes the Core (*Organization Foundation*), a Support Layer (*Departments/Areas*) and an External Layer (*Projects*).

The Core, which is the organization's answers to the Formula For Intentionality. Why does it exist, where is it going, how will it get there and within what guidelines?

We want our Core strong and deeply anchored. Auditing the Core assesses its strength and accuracy. We follow a process to determine how strong it is. Where elements of the Core are missing, broken, or wrong, we'll rectify.

The Support Layers (*areas or departments*) is how we segment our organization so we can easily delegate categories of authority to operate within our organizational structure. We evaluate the structure of the department, its goals, and strategies while restraining from diving deep through individual projects.

The External layer (*Projects*) is how we segment our departments into tactical actions. These projects directly address a specific gap and are crucial to bringing the vision of an organization to life.

Once we know where we're auditing, we take that section of the organization through three audit levels.

The Painting Of Three Portraits

Our first stage in the audit process involves painting the portrait of our past, the portrait of our present, and the portrait we want from our future.

Our past gives us insight into our origin and from where we came. It also allows us to learn how we succeeded and how we failed. These lessons are invaluable as we move forward.

With a clear picture of the present, it allows us to see how we've changed from where we started. It also gives us our starting point for moving towards our desired future outcome.

Our vision pulls the appropriate actions required for our expected future state. The contrast between the present and the future allows us to see and prioritize the gaps so we can effectively arrive at our destination.

The following actionable audit process is designed to make this easier to follow while also delivering clear actions to move your business forward.

The Five Phases To Transition Your Organization

Most tangled organizations are struggling and don't have the luxury to start over from scratch. Often, money is tight, and they need some quick wins. The following strategy is designed to help provide fast gains that help justify the subsequent steps.

Many visionary small business owners will want to quickly go to step four, skipping the highly necessary first three steps.

But don't. Stop yourself. Be disciplined and let your team and friends hold you accountable.

Let's revisit the five steps to untangle the mess and move towards an organized and streamlined operation.

1. Tackle low hanging fruit (*high impact, low effort*)
2. Simplify everything (*cut, consolidate, and shrink*)
3. Make what's left better
4. Identify & fill in the gaps (*what's missing?*)

5. Master maintenance (*from our strong foundation*)

As you consider the strategy most applicable to your organization today, let's explore each element starting with our early wins.

And, while I'll explain each step and share a few examples, this process will be uniquely tailored to your situation. It'll be up to you to apply the concepts and flesh out the details of what they mean in your business.

Phase 1 - Tackle Low Hanging Fruit (*Quickly*)

When first working with clients, I immediately look for high impact low effort (*how I define low hanging fruit*)

endeavors to tackle. These early wins fuel our future efforts, buy us time and cultivates trust with others.

It's hard to make broad sweeping improvements in an organization that doesn't have an immediate return. Establishing a track record of early and easy successes builds trust with your team empowering you to ask for more dramatic changes that require more time to bear fruit.

On the practical side of things, we also want these wins to generate revenue, increase conversions, or help us better deliver on what we're selling. If we're making more money and our efforts are a significant contributor, getting more resources is no longer an issue. These early wins fund the next steps in the process.

Key Question

- What are some actions you and your team could take today that could have a dramatic positive impact within the next 30-60 days?

Phase 2 - Simplify Everything

> *"Devoting a little of yourself to everything means committing a great deal of yourself to nothing." - Andy Stanley*

It's bizarre (*but easily understood, and possibly part of our DNA*) how many small business owners overcommit. They're doing more than they could ever realistically accomplish even in an ideal scenario.

I was in this very situation with my marketing company, and it's where most visionaries find themselves — Saying yes to everything and no to nothing.

What were we thinking (*or not*)?

Burning ourselves and other people out was no longer a viable strategy for building our business. This insanity had to stop, and we began intentionally abandoning and retiring things we couldn't fulfill with excellence.

In other cases, we merged multiple like projects to prevent waste and foster a more streamlined approach. We sought to find ways to change how we're doing what we're doing, making it easier and faster to manage well. **As much as we did this, it was still hard for me to let these ideas and projects go. Visionaries want it all.**

My current freelancing business is an excellent example of '*Simplify Everything.*' I ended the marketing company and isolated it down to a focused set of services within a set amount of guidelines. I now manage less, have more impact, earn more income, and work fewer hours. I do more with less, and it's incredible.

What if you could shrink your business operations, manage less responsibility, make more money, have more time with family, and do the things you love? This potential is what's at stake by not simplifying everything.

Only do what makes progress towards the end game (*which means you need to know the vision*).

What, in your business, could be dramatically simplified, so it's easier to manage and easier to make progress?

Phase 3 - Make What's Left Better

Making things better requires intention and energy. The reason we simplify everything before this stage is because we want to minimize the number of things we're going to improve. Since we usually lack resources, operating within our limitations is key to our long-term success. So the less we're required to manage, the better.

Actions, projects, and people that made it past the simplify everything campaign now become our focus. Our mission now is to make the things we've kept as impressive as they can be. However we can leverage them to our benefit, we will.

By earning some quick wins and simplifying everything, we're energized and equipped for this stage. With less to focus on and more resources to dedicate, we can do things that were impossible to do before the big audit.

We'll also continue organizing what we're keeping around, so we accurately and easily see the gaps and missing pieces in the next phase.

What if you created everything with excellence? What if you were looked up to as a shining example?

By making what's left better, you'll be knocking it out of the park on the things you've justified keeping around.

What's something worth focusing on that could be made better within your organization?

Phase 4 - Identify & Fill The Gaps

After making what's left better, we should have excellent visibility on our portfolio of actions, projects, processes, and people. By completing the previous phase, we've also established the standard of excellence we'll adhere to as we fill the gaps.

Now, we survey the landscape to identify what we're missing and how we'll go about filling these gaps. This step of the process is a deliberate one where we scan each area of the business to discover what essential elements are missing. We want to find things we need or will make us stronger. But, they must build on what we've done so far, not distract us (*don't get tangled again!*).

With one of my clients, we've gotten the blog archives organized, consolidated, and merged, so we can see which blogs posts to create in the future for completing our collection. And a *"completed collection"* is a good symbol for understanding when we've finished this phase four of the transitory process.

What if you found and took advantage of every opportunity solidly and effectively across the board? What if you had little to no blind spots in your business?

Filling in all the gaps moves us toward this type of strength.

Where are the problematic gaps in your organization? What are you going to do about filling them?

Phase 5 - From This Foundation, Master Maintenance & Grow The Company

When we arrive at this step, we've completed a great accomplishment. It's a powerful feeling to transform an existing business in such a dramatic way. It's this new foundation which will act as our springboard to new and fantastic business growth.

From a solid and deliberately created foundation and framework, we leverage our positioning and approach to scale our efforts speedily. With these first four stages preparing the rocket for space, this phase is where we launch out of the atmosphere to space and beyond.

But, while we continue to create new things along the way, we can maintain with excellence over a long period that establishes the compounding growth we hope and expect.

Going forward, we only create what we can make better and what makes us better are the numerous little iterative improvements. Daily pushes of our twenty-mile march build momentum over days, weeks, months, and years, leading to dramatic business transformation for the history books.

The key here is to steadily sustain what we have, understand the core systems required to make our business work, and always be looking for ways to make them better. Be careful not to get distracted with other shiny objects; otherwise, you'll quickly find yourself back where you started.

Fall In Love With The Process Required To Sustain Your Business

In the Greek mythological story of Sisyphus, the king of Ephyra is punished by the gods for overly promoting himself as powerful and vital, and for his greedy and deceptive nature. For eternity, he's forced to roll an immense boulder up a hill only for it to roll back down when it nears the top. For all time, he's cursed to push and re-push the rock up the mountain.

I can relate.

When owning and operating Noodlehead Marketing, I felt this burden, specifically when it came to our new project sales. To survive (*make payroll, among other things*) required a large amount of effort each month. It was brutal and a process that consistently overwhelmed me.

Accepting how life works is our stepping stone out of the curse. For visionaries who hate the mundane, this drudgery is the path out of the eternal cycle.

When I was young, my generous father would incentivize me to write book reports by giving me five dollars for each book read with an essay to compliment. I'd knock out these books and reports as quickly as I possibly could, and would never look back. He encouraged me to re-read my essays to correct all the errors and make the report better. But whether it was the report or any school work, this review was something I despised doing and resisted when he required it for my five dollars. I didn't care for the process. All I wanted was the result.

Now, when it comes to writing, I love the process. This work includes writing, editing, publishing, and celebration. Whether it's an email, a blog post, or this book, I'm reading and re-rereading it over and over until it flows and moves how I want it. While I don't dwell on it being perfect, I want it to be excellent. And the process to get there may seem mundane, but because I value and enjoy it (*in addition to the result*), I don't see it as a punishment. I've transformed my curse into a blessing.

So, what if you found love for the process of pushing the boulder up the hill? What if you came to appreciate the process and details that make your business work at a fundamental level?

You'd go from being cursed to push the rock up the hill to loving the grind of doing it. But, it'd require you run the type of business where you got excited about the process of creating, doing, and maintaining. And, that you removed everything else.

We find long-term sustained success on the other side of mastering maintenance. To live and work in a cycle of sustainability, and to love (*or at least value*) each step of the process is paramount. When you learn to enjoy turning the flywheel each day, not only will it reveal and develop your character, it'll move you towards the destination you've strived for all these years.

It Takes Time, But You Can Make It Happen

Depending on the size and complexity of your company's tangled web will determine how long this five-phase transitory process will take. Expect several years to go through the first four steps and live into the fifth.

By following the steps in this transition process, you'll have a long-lasting business and a powerful sense of accomplishment as you build and sustain the growth of your organization.

But, while this process is effective at untangling your company, the most important lesson is to prevent yourself from falling right back into this chaos.

Carrying IDEMA Forward, When You're In The Master Maintenance Phase

Remember IDEMA. And build your systems around the framework or a likewise alternative that considers all five areas.

1. A way to capture and catalog ideas.
2. A place and process to move these ideas forward and plan for their execution.
3. An effective team of people who can bring these ideas to life.
4. A culture of maintenance, where projects are not simply launched and abandoned but cared for like a garden, which our life depends on.
5. A cadence of review and reflection to ensure we're always moving forward and growing, and never stagnating or bloating.

When you unravel your business and sustain an IDEMA ecosystem, you'll be set to get to your final destination. And while it may be hard for you, a small business owner, to go at it slowly and surely, it's necessary. And, to prevent the embroiled small business, requires doing it organically.

The Value Of Organically Growing Our Business

I've been working with business owners for over a decade in a variety of contexts, and one common denominator I've come across is the drive to artificially accelerate the growth of the business by skipping the planning phase, leveraging debt, and living off of comfortable income streams. Yes, I've done all three, and could easily fall back into any of them. These become a barrier between what we know we should do, and what we do.

When business owners get ahead of themselves, they miss the beauty and valuable lessons that come with intentional organic growth.

Organic growth presents a pathway of what we need to do now, and what we need to do next. It fosters the ability for us to walk in the light we have and not get ahead of ourselves. Since visionary business owners tend to operate so futuristically, it's the slow, methodical organic process they usually need help doing.

During my freelancing journey, I've experienced how powerful this process of organic growth plays out.

Two examples include shifting away from fixed pricing when I first started freelancing, and towards billing my clients on an hourly basis in batches of ten hours (*the BAM system is a hit!*).

As a result of charging hourly, I have a finite amount of time to offer clients, leading to my three goals every month (*adjusted for hourly rates across years*).

- Less than 80 hours/month = Red, Surviving
- Between 81-108 hours = Yellow, Good
- More than 109 hours = Green, Great

One hundred forty-nine adjusted hours (*one hundred and nineteen actual hours in 2018*) is my super-green goal. It is my maximum standard capacity and the top of the green zone.

While I started freelancing in 2014, It wasn't until a year later that I started tracking my hours in a way that would allow me to see my progress or regress over time. In the following graph, you'll see my freelancing starts at a low level.

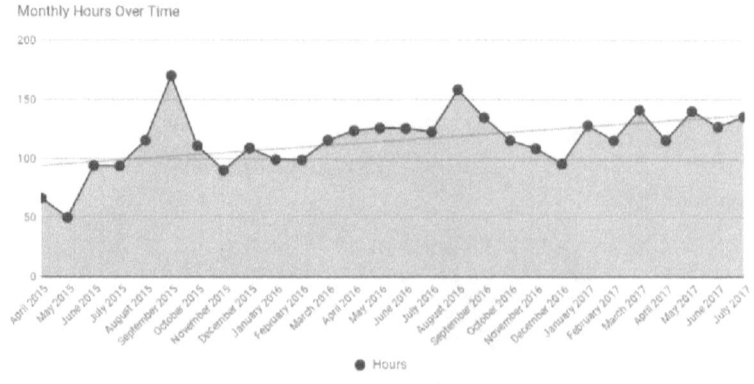

This shift was a drop from several fairly good months prior. It was during that valley that my water tower system (*financial buffer, see Path of the Freelancer*) became our lifesaver during a challenging personal season. As I rolled into 2016, I hit a level of steadiness in middle green. As I launched in 2017, I hit a level of steady high green. And this continued through 2018/19.

My Yearly Averages

- 2014 | Monthly average = 80 hours
- 2015 | Monthly average = 100 hours
- 2016 | Monthly average = 127 hours*
- 2017 | Monthly average = 147 hours*
- 2018 | Monthly average = 144 hours*

hour counts normalized with hourly rate increase adjustment

How Organic Growth Unfolded For Me

My first goal towards organic growth was to stay out of the red zone. In the first year, there were months when I was out of it, and months where I was in the red. It was much more sporadic, but this roller coaster led to creating a personal, responsive budget that could adapt as our income did.

In 2015, I put the pedal to the metal to make steady green happen. It also resulted in my most substantial number of hours in one month ever, which helped pull my yearly averages towards green.

During 2017, I had the opportunity to get more organized and structured with my freelancing business. I set up new accounting and time tracking tools. I got more focused on reviewing my daily, weekly, monthly, and annual reports. Ultimately, I laid the foundation to succeed at the highest level.

To rewind for a moment, in 2016, I launched from the well-grounded foundation towards continued steady growth in high green. In July 2016, I increased (*for the first time*) my hourly rate from $75/hour to $80/hour as I was close to hitting capacity.

During that extra time, I took the systems I created and began migrating them into better tools to do the job. I built an Airtable dashboard for my freelancing work. It tracks my hours, income, clients, projects, payroll, and a variety of other things. I also set up small automation tasks to free up some of my time.

In 2017, my goal was to sustain high green hours each month for the duration of the year. At the beginning of the year, I increased my rate again from $80/hour to $85/hour. While my first increase in pricing led to a downtick in the number of hours, the second increase led to an uptick in quantity.

With such a high volume of projects in 2017, I had to learn new strategies and tactics to help me manage and execute well.

Another huge leap in 2017 was switching accounting systems to Harpoon (*the excellent example company I praised earlier*). Our philosophy and approach to financial management for freelancers is closely aligned. Switching over to their system removed additional friction.

Organically Moving Forward

In 2018, my goal was increasing my rate again with the intent to sustain the same income while also decreasing the number of hours I work per month. This approach also involved a strategy of creating products that generate revenue without my time (*including this book*).

I now have a handle on how well I'm doing and my capacity. This clarity motivates me to push forward while also throttling back, so I don't drive so far that I burn myself out. (*Yeah, I still seem to do that at times*)

While this journey of freelancing is organically playing out and because I don't have a company I'm managing, **I get the pleasing opportunity to watch the various little details that are usually ignored and passed over by business owners.**

It reminds me of the childhood game, Jenga. Playing the block-stacking game fast and without care usually leads to an unbalanced tower and quicker ending. This approach is easily how building a business can easily play out.

But, if instead I slowly and methodically remove bricks and place them higher, I can ensure a stronger, more stable, and extended game. (*That's about where this metaphor ends, and tragedy begins, haha!*)

Going slowly and deliberately provides the opportunity to see the next strategic move. It allows us to test, practice, and master it. Doing so gives us a stronger foundation from which to build.

As a movie extra on American Made (*with Tom Cruise*), I met a fellow extra and aspiring actor on set who said people fall as quickly as they rise to fame. He chose to take the extended and steady road to acting success, so when his career finally comes to an end, it'll be an extended transition, not a trip off a cliff (*like many one-hit wonders*).

At this season of my life with the responsibilities I've got, I prefer to adopt this slow and steady approach toward my future. It's a lot slower than I'd prefer, but I recognize my family, and I will be much better off because of it.

A Simple Project Management System To Manage This Process

While IDEMA is a terrific framework for looking at and organizing a business, it can seem ambiguous with the specific details of how to organize and make stuff happen.

To compensate for this here's a highly practical structure undergirded by IDEMA, but uninhibited by its limitations for project management. This system is designed to be structured enough to provide order, but as frictionless as possible for effectively and directly managing numerous projects.

Using Airtable, a spreadsheet, kanban board, or notepad, create a list with a status column. This status column includes the following orderly sequence.

- Done
- Maintain
- Stuck
- Active
- Next
- Idea Repository
- Archive

As you get ideas, add them and place them in the idea repository status (*with Airtable, you can easily group these in order*). When you want to work on the next one, or are actively working on them now, update their status accordingly. *Stuck* is obvious. When you have a recurring action or project, move it to *Maintain* status. *Done* is for one-and-done actions and projects, and is a helpful grouping for reporting.

The order is essential because we want to focus on the top down. When the top is short of items, it's time to move lower items up the totem pole hierarchy.

Name	Status	Passengers
Blog Post	Done	Cris
Send Email	Stuck	Ellen
Hire CMO	Active	Keith
Upgrade ECP	Next	Craig

With the first column, label the items by name, the second will label the status; we'll create a third called *Passengers*. This class is a multi-select field for listing all the people involved at the current stage. You can also add a note field, and other columns to help specify the details.

And that's it. Keep the list updated and move items through it. If you're using Airtable, filter out items in the archive category and when you've finished, reported, or abandoned something, archive it, and it'll disappear from your view.

If you're organizing a complicated project or department, add columns to deal with the different departments, projects, and ideas. Alternatively, explore a sophisticated project management system like *Basecamp*.

Memorializing The Small Business Transformation Process From Chaos To Clarity

Ideally, we prevent a chaotic and rogue oriented business from ever happening in the first place, but the reality is that most of us won't. And, sometimes this rogue approach is the very thing needed to pioneer in an uncertain and competitive marketplace.

But, it should be our mission to translate that chaos towards a state of order. That is where to find the value and where we maximize profit.

And, you're good at it already. If you couldn't do this well, you wouldn't have a business. The challenge is not merely knowing what to do. The problem is accepting what's required to sustain it, and recognizing that the gap lies between what you know and what you do (*or don't*).

Each time you fall back into a chaotic state for your business, and you implement the five steps to get reorganized and oriented towards what matters most, remember the work required to do it. And remember how much easier it would have been to prevent tangling up in the first place.

It's not until you're sick and tired of this cycle and able to accept the cold hard reality of the better way that it will genuinely solidify a change in your trajectory.

We don't change until our current context pushes us out or a new one entices us with something better (*or both*).

If the time for permanent, sustainable change is now, and you're finally ready, the Jump is for you. If you still think there's another way, other than the hard option you keep passing by season after season as you chase shiny objects, place this book on your shelf and revisit it when that approach doesn't work out for you.

The Jump will patiently wait.

Remember IDEMA, The Framework For Capturing & Sustaining Ideas

My goal is to brand IDEMA (*Ideate, Discover, Execute, Maintain, & Audit*) deep into your subconscious and to have you slightly annoyed with me for how often I talk about it (*how close are we?*).

The five stages for transforming your small business from chaos to order are a way to unravel the messiness of your business into a clear and manageable structure. But, it's a transformational process to take you from where you are to where you want to be. It's not enough to carry you forward when completed.

Ongoing sustainability falls on the IDEMA framework. **Entrench it in your mindset, business structure, and organizational processes.**

Capture and prioritize ideas. Explore and plan them. Execute the best ones and those you finish, and expect to sustain them. Maintain excellence and regularly review what you're doing to make it better. Deeply root this into every facet of your business.

Bring In The Audit

Embrace the audit process. Regularly be asking why you're doing what you're doing, and in that assessment conclude one of the following three outcomes.

Do we keep as is? Change it for the better? Or stop altogether?

Apply this mindset to your organization as a whole, each department, and the individual projects. And, use the five-phase process to streamline the process and produce results through the transition to justify the subsequent actions.

And after you've made improvements, give yourself time to see the results.

The Chaos to Clarity Process

When you're feeling overwhelmed or uncertain where to start, and what to do next, this transitional audit process is what you need. In fact, for many, it's intuitive and you likely already have followed a similar one when you've faced the harsh challenges of growing a business.

When cash flow comes crunching in, and sales are declining, we find focus and clarity real quick.

To equip you in proactively preventing these moments of crisis, remember and use the five stages of transition. While the order is essential, there will be moments required to go rogue and change up the order. But like rolling a tube of toothpaste to get it all out, don't skip the stages. You'll need them all.

1. Tackle high impact, low effort actions.
2. Simplify everything.
3. Make the rest better.
4. Fill in the gaps.
5. Master sustainability.

When I'm working with clients through this process, often they don't know or are so panicked they can't think straight. But, those top phases set the foundation to establish and grow trust. They generate the results required to ensure that the remainder of the process does not get neglected.

Organic Business Growth

Until you've mastered the launch, growth, and maintenance of business creation several times, a slower, more deliberate approach is what's needed. It's how we fully understand each aspect of the process. When we've fully understood it, we can explore how best to accelerate and scale.

Until then, accept and lean into the slow and steady growth pathway. This season of learning and care to the details is a significant factor in equipping you to overcome the obstacles preventing your success.

The key indicator to know when you have mastered it comes down to how often you can replicate success. If you're merely a one-hit wonder, you were likely riding more on luck and someone else's performance.

Practical Application

Ultimately, please keep it simple and practical. As a creative person myself, I can easily float away into the clouds of possibility and metaphor. While that can be helpful at times, it's where the rubber meets the road that matters most.

Make your efforts real, and use project management tools to track and execute the things that matter most. And harness the level of accountability necessary to push you past your fail points. Please don't leave it up to your historical patterns of chronic abandonment.

11. My Parting Words To The Visionary Business Owner

> *"Truth - more precisely, an accurate understanding of reality - is the essential foundation for producing good outcomes." - Ray Dalio, Principles: Life & Work*

For you and your small business, I want clarity because that clarity is your starting point for moving towards what you want, from and out of your business. But while you need and want clarity, it's chaos that surrounds you (*and much of it caused by your own doing directly or indirectly*).

While facing and transitioning out of chaos during the halfway point of my small business journey, a strong visual metaphor came to me (*mentioned earlier*), helping to understand what was going on and why the clarity and order were so impactful.

In this visual, I imagined a messy house. Clutter filled every room with stuff and garbage. Chaos was everywhere.

Chaos burns out and ejects your people, especially the good ones. You find you have good ideas and structure in your head, but your team is not on the same wavelength. This discord causes unnecessary stress-inducing tension.

You are likely starting and launching many new ideas with little or no consideration for how you'll keep those ideas going. With poor follow up, they quickly fade into the background when your excitement for them disappears, or something more interesting comes along. Looking back, you see a corridor of broken promises and forgotten dreams for you and those who follow.

Ultimately, you have too many activities and responsibilities. You and your small business are bloated. In effect, change and innovation are slow or non-existent. You can't get anywhere, and you move nowhere. And like the messy metaphorical house, your small business is a mess, filled with chaos.

But like me, you may wonder what in the world is causing all this chaos? And that is our first vital problem to accept and tackle. **Find the source of the chaos.**

Unfortunately, since our metaphorical house is in turmoil, it's almost impossible to see where the problem is, and what is driving it.

The key? Getting cleaned and organized so you can isolate the root of what's causing the problem.

Enter, IDEMA. Structure. Order. Visibility. Accountability. When our house is in order, we can see when things crop up, problems arise, and the source of it becomes quite clear.

Our indecisiveness and procrastination quickly come to the surface. Our unresolved history and traumatic life experiences are driving us to cultivate the chaos as a way to cope with the pain and suffering we feel. Like a warm blanket making a child feel safe, chaos covers us and helps us feel better (*falsely*).

And it's in this visual house metaphor that I came to realize there was a monster in my metaphorical basement, something inside of me with long tentacles causing the chaos. My insecurities. My fears. My masked hopes and dreams. And left unchecked, this inner monster grows and takes over our entire house.

We've pushed this truth off because our monster is scary.

But, it's time for you to lean in, to face these things you're hiding from, and avoiding. **It won't be easy, but if you're sick and tired of the cycle and want to make progress (*instead of wandering in circles*), it's time for you to act.**

If you want visibility of what work your team is doing, and you value having a common language, then take the step. Dig deep and face yourself. And as part of the process, you'll need to clean house and to stay organized, so you can see the chaos erupt when it does. And in doing so, you'll begin to see what's causing the mess in your life and small business.

But know this, what's causing the chaos is not something we vanquish, and it's gone forever. It's a mindset that recognizes we must face and destroy it while keeping our foot on its throat as long as we're alive.

It reminds me of the new treatments for HIV. There is a drug people with this virus can take that will suppress the virus so much, it's as if they don't have the disease. They can take a blood test, and they'll come back clean. They cannot infect others as an unmedicated carrier would. For all practical purposes, they can live a regular life. But, they must always take the medicine. They are forever dependent on this life-saving pill to save their lives and allow them to live. Within a short period of not using the medication, the virus comes back to destroy.

In the same way, this is true for us small business owners. We can implement the order, face conflict and challenges head-on, deal with our issues, and lead others courageously, but we must remember, this is an ongoing battle that does not end. Entropy has no mercy.

But, by embracing clarity and order, we will find it's much easier to manage (*once we get past the effects of our fostered chaos*) than the overwhelming chaos we've created (*and allowed*) in our business.

So, what are you going to do? Keep hiding, or step out and into the challenge?

Let's Talk About The Realities You're Facing

You're out of steam. There's too much to do. And you're falling further behind every day.

And it feels like the same story every year. Well, at least for a handful of the previous years.

Did you go into business to operate this way? Is this how you imagined entrepreneurship would unfold? Has the chaos become comfortable?

What if your small business could provide for you and your team, be enjoyable, have meaning, and facilitate ongoing success?

All at the same time?

That's what you want. That's what I wanted. That's what we can have. It's what we would have, but something's missing.

But, there's a way to find that missing ingredient, likely several of them. And it's the process shared earlier for making the jump (*chaos to order*). Let's see it one more time.

The Five-Stage Process To Untangle Your Business And Move It, Forward

Leaders are repeaters, and what's most important is said throughout the Jump book many many times. This process is one of them. Here's the quick and dirty rundown of the five stages to move you from chaos to order.

1. Tackle low effort high impact endeavors.
2. Simplify everything everywhere.
3. Make what's left better.
4. Identify and fill in the gaps to effectively move forward.
5. Master sustainability.

Take the process, overlay it with your business, and see where you stumble. Where do you struggle, and where do you stop?

Following the process will illuminate the missing pieces in you as a leader, the holes in your business foundation, the team members you've left behind, and the lack of systems to scale your operation.

Ultimately, face and embrace the reality of what it takes to run a well-oiled machine as a business, and ask yourself a fundamental question.

Is this the business you want to place all your effort? It's going to be hard, so is this worth it?

During the final year of Noodlehead Marketing, I had a clear choice in front of me. Rebooting the company was going to be hard. Sustaining that business the right way would be challenging. Knowing I'd focus this energy towards something in my life, was my marketing agency going to be the target of this effort?

My answer was no. My yes was elsewhere. So, I let go of what was in front of me, something that was great in numerous ways, to go a different direction.

For you, it may be yes. But the clarity of that yes imbued with the harsh reality of business ownership, and the success that comes from the required responsibility will set the foundation to do what's required; **to say no to everything except the one thing you've answered yes.**

Stop RAMming Things (*Rogue Action Management*) & Start Leveraging System Oriented Leadership (SOL)

From your strong commitment flows the ingredients to build a long-lasting foundation for your company.

When numerous opportunities flow your way, you'll confidently say no without fear of missing out on something good. Because what's most significant is what you're going after. Nothing else matters, and the distractions that so easily pulled you away from your focus have no sway from your direction. You're in it to the end, and to do it right.

You'll take your time building actively from the foundation, fostering an abundance of margin — your anchoring into bedrock and setting this up for the long run.

Short-term wins are nice, but they're merely you taking advantage of the opportunities that have displayed themselves in front of you while also moving towards the larger goal. It's the long-term wins you're most interested in harnessing. If a short-term opportunity can pull you away, it's an easy and resounding no.

You're a strong leader now. And, where you're not, your aware of and working on it. You've built teams and systems to augment your weaknesses and amplify you and your team's strengths.

Everything done has an intent, and everyone knows how every action plays into the broader mission. What is done today, matters, because it changes the trajectory and pace of the company.

Communication is so proactive and precise; it's as if you and your team are reading each other's minds.

People are devastated, leaving the organization, because of how powerfully positive their involvement has become.

This scenario is the end game.

And it's something we can all create if we choose to.

But it goes back to accepting reality and choosing where to focus.

Are you ready for them both?

Remember & Systematize IDEMA For Everything You Care About

When we don't see the full lifecycle of how things unfold, we're inclined to make poor decisions. We lose ideas, never plan, fail to execute, neglect maintenance, and forget to audit. When this is your approach towards business, you are toast.

In the first several years of Noodlehead Marketing, I felt as if something was missing from my toolkit. Companies had systems, processes, and people, but what held it all together? What brought cohesion to all these disparate parts working in different directions? If this cohesion is simply a person, they become a bottleneck, so there must be a stronger and better option.

It took me time to find and articulate it, but this is the problem IDEMA seeks to solve, and where it's power shines. This framework is the underlying structure of your business. Every idea, project, department, and organization goes through a life cycle, and IDEMA illuminates it practically.

At the base level, IDEMA reminds me to capture ideas, plan out my intentions for those ideas, execute the plan we've created, and to consider what's required to keep it alive indefinitely.

And finally, IDEMA informs me that at some point, I need to reflect and find out if we keep going as is, change course, or stop altogether. And this insight is critical if we're to align ourselves with the truth of how things happen.

Ideally, you systematize this framework in how you structure your company, and how you lead others. The iceberg of unknowns can go deep, but we often limit ourselves by not systematically exploring the expected and potential knowns and unknowns.

Your unrealistic visions are grand, but making them happen must be grounded in how you bring them to life. So as you continue building your business, always remember IDEMA. Moreover, build it, your team, and your processes around it.

1. **Ideate**. Capture our idea.
2. **Discover**. Establish intentions & plan to sustain.
3. **Execute**. Start, finish, and prepare to maintain.
4. **Maintain**. Sustain our idea.
5. **Audit**. Determine our assessed idea's fate.

The deeper entrenched it goes into your mind, leadership, and operations, the more effective you'll become in growing your organization, and fostering an environment of flourishing. And if you need to build your framework, because you're a creator like me, then start now.

12. Standing On The Edge

Here you are.

On the edge of the chasm, you are looking out across the expanse, towards what seems like an impossible jump.

You've failed before.

The pressure is pushing in on you. Will it be different this time?

If you're going to give it everything you've got, it better be a business you can commit to fully. Is ending the journey your next step? Turn around now. Find your true mission.

If forward is where you belong, the right preparation and approach to the Jump will give you what's required to finish what you started.

Before making the leap and transforming your business, remember the four steps required to give you the lift necessary to make your landing.

A new & better business requires...

- *... a transformed leader.*
- *... a strong business foundation.*
- *... your dedicated team.*
- *... bulletproof systems & mental models.*

Take the preceding four steps, and then...

Go make the jump.

For a free printable download of all the key questions found throughout the book, go to JasonScottMontoya.com/jump

Epilogue By My Friend, A Small Business Owner

After thirteen years of growth, my business plateaued for five years. I was burned out and constantly looking for the exit (*Is this where you find yourself?*).

Halfway to my office, the day after learning my line of credit was in jeopardy, I turned a corner (*figuratively speaking*) — It was a moment so profound that the location was branded into my mind. Like the main character in a movie, I suddenly found the strength and endurance needed to finish the mission.

"**NO!** This is **MY** business. I started it, and I know how to **FIX** it".

I decided at that moment that I was not a victim; I could figure this out, and I'd get us to where we were going.

Truthfully, I didn't know what to do. But most importantly, I was willing to do what was necessary, no matter how difficult.

I decided: "I'll do whatever it takes".

I'll move past the emotion of tough decisions, change the way we're doing things, give people role clarity, let the wrong people go, shut down irrelevant aspects of the business; whatever it takes.

This monumental moment for business owners is perhaps a necessary event for us all.

Operating from a nearby coffee shop (*instead of the office*), I focused **ON** the business instead of working **IN** it. This incidental and monumental shift is now a vital leadership practice in my business.

We quickly changed our overhead structure, pulling together a survival plan for better cash flow (*tackle low effort, high impact low hanging fruit, and simplify everything*). To buy us time and give us breathing room, I brought in new working capital through a short-term loan. Looking for cost savings, I also dove into every expense line item.

What we did during our five years of financial stagnation obviously wasn't working, so with margin in place, I dedicated time thinking and praying about how we'd proceed (*reflecting back, and looking forward*).

One of the **VERY** first things I did was build a daily routine of foundational activities for success; praying, journaling, reading, and reviewing an ever-evolving set of quotes and statements that shape how I view the company and want others to see the business (*like core values, leadership quotes, and other important insights*).

I also realized my leadership team slowly disappeared over the five previous years, and I didn't fully value or utilize them when they were in place. My current people were floundering across the business with confusing or missing job descriptions, and there were significant KPI (*key performance indicators*) gaps. There was disorder and a lack of accountability and structure in the business. No wonder we weren't going anywhere.

Have you heard the saying, *"You can't see the forest for the trees"?*

Hindsight is 20/20, but when you're in it and learning, you don't see so clearly. Often we have to *"feel our way through it"*. For the first thirteen years in business, we were *"accidentally and entrepreneurially successful."* I stumbled upon opportunities and built a business around what I intuitively saw to do. This is often the *"recipe"* for how entrepreneurs launch their company. And this mindset was something inside me that had to change (*building a better business requires leveling up as a leader*).

Over the subsequent months, I stabilized the business and quickly realized there were three major areas for improvement.

1. Defining a vision for where we were going (*as part of our strong business foundation*).

2. Creating company-wide role clarity (*to empower my loyal team*).

3. Building a leadership team (*so I can better share responsibility*).

What's worth doing is rarely easy, and these three initiatives are no exception. Compound the difficulty of

DOING the work with **AFFORDING** the people, and it quickly gets daunting. Against the alternative of giving up, I promptly decided to put in the worthwhile hard work required.

This change in my business started with **ME**, and my willingness to understand and live out my role as the company leader. This means leaning into the advice and accountability of advisors and peers. It also requires spending the **TIME** necessary to think and pray about the business.

What's working and needs to continue, what's broken that needs fixing, and **WHO** needs to be **WHERE** doing **WHAT**? (*like Jason's audit process*)

There is **ONE** chief leader in business, and that person is there for a reason. The reason we stalled out for five years is that I was neglecting my leadership role. We accidentally and entrepreneurially succeeded for many easy years. But as things changed, I never did (*fossilizing, as Jason puts it*). It wasn't until I let things get so bad that I was forced to face and address my lack of role effectiveness as the leader.

We are now stronger, have leaders in several key positions, role clarity across numerous jobs, and we've completed significant work on a compelling vision. I'm grateful for how far we've come, even though there is (*always*) plenty more to do.

One instrumental element in creating role clarity, KPI's, and ultimately sustainability is our **VAS System** (**V**isibility and **A**ccountability creates **S**ustainability). To produce the desired results requires knowing and seeing what must happen like clockwork (*maintain service levels, customer* *service, stock or sales levels, etc.*). Monitored, consistent, and well-executed actions are likely to produce expected results.

As part of rolling out our VAS System, we chose these points of clarity and created *Visibility* (*charts / dashboards / reporting*) and *Accountability (role clarity, KPI's*) which increased the *Sustainability* of our desired outcomes. In a similar way to how Jason sees and uses IDEMA and the Business Blueprint, I leverage the VAS System.

Business, more than anything, is a system of processes. Figure out what they are for **YOUR** business, get the **RIGHT** people responsible for the **RIGHT** things. Spend time keeping leaders out of the ditch and supplying them with what they need to be successful (*vision, funding, encouragement, advice, and coaching*).

Nothing worth doing is easy, so don't decide your future path based purely on the level of difficulty. If, upon reflection, you decide **THIS** business is worthy of a significant part of your life, spend the time to figure out your system of processes, get the right people accountable for the right things, and **JUMP**!

Your best future awaits you.

> *Craig is the founder and CEO of **CablesAndKits.com**, a distributor and retailer of network hardware and cabling infrastructure. Connect with Craig at linkedin.com/in/craighaynie.*

Acknowledgments

I could not have completed this book without the help and support of those I love and who love me.

We thrive together.

Thank you, Jesus, for the love, grace, and the opportunity provided for me to write The Jump. The abundance of provision, support, insights, and community was invaluable in completing this task.

Thank you to my lovely and enduring wife, and all five loving and giving children, Madison, David, Judah, Elihu, and Zoë. I appreciate your sacrifice, in time and focus, as I wrote this book.

Thank you, Cris Anzai, for being the first to read the book in its entirety, and providing a range of helpful feedback to make the book better.

Thank you, Craig Haynie, for writing the introduction and epilogue, being a great friend, and participating in a part of my freelancing success as a client.

Thank you, Ellen Bristol, Keith Eigel, Toby Bloomberg, David Cline, Todd Wahl, Jason Shinn, Sobem Nwoko, Addison Williams, Eva Miles, Jeremy Sloan, Andy Johnson, and John Lehmberg for providing feedback to make the book stronger.

Thank you, Jim Karwisch, for your friendship, time discussing the concepts in this book, helping to make the cover better, and for sharing life with me.

Thank you, Len Wikberg and Beth Coetzee, for your friendship, insights, and support during the years of Noodlehead Marketing. Much of what is in this book came from our journey together.

Thank you to all who shared a small insight or feedback for making the book better.

IDEMA is a system for capturing and bringing ideas to life, a set of processes for excellence and accountability, and a box of tools for effective business operations. It was birthed out of Noodlehead Marketing.

Learn more and explore project management resources at the dedicated IDEMA page.

https://medium.com/@IDEMA

The Jump Next Steps

1. Business Growth Blogging

Did you personally and professionally connect with the content in this book? Are you interested in continuing the journey to grow yourself, your business, and your community?

Check out my website and blog, and be sure to sign up for email updates to ensure you keep the process going. *www.jasonscottmontoya.com*

2. Consulting Services

Did you find the content in this book relevant, compelling, and helpful? Are you interested in continuing the journey through a paid engagement?

Let's talk. Visit my services page at the following link to learn more before reaching out. *www.jasonscottmontoya.com/work*

3. Speaking Engagements

Are you interested in sharing the concepts and stories from this book to your group, company, or conference?

Let's discuss. Explore the following link to learn more before reaching out. *https://www.jasonscottmontoya.com/speaking*

About The Author

Jason Scott Montoya is a creative entrepreneur who grows small business owners, teams, and incomes around the Atlanta, Georgia area.

As a fifth-generation business owner who works with entrepreneurs, he knows what it's like to launch, build, and sustain a small business. It's no easy task, and often a lonely road. But working together (*or reading this book*) you get a helpful coach to encourage you forward, while also specifically addressing the pressing challenges you're currently facing.

Beyond reading this book, you can also follow along on his blog — *www.jasonscottmontoya.com* — where he shares stories and systems to live better and work smarter.

A follower of the WAY, the Truth, & the Life, Jason lives with his wife and five children.

Path Of The Freelancer

Freelancing Is Difficult. Are You Ready For This Rewarding Challenge?

After the shut down of his marketing firm, Jason Scott Montoya unexpectedly had numerous business owners and non-profit leaders requesting his help to solve their organization's communication problems.

Facing numerous challenges as a new freelancer, he quickly integrated his business insights to move through the many familiar obstacles he faced. He then began sharing with other freelancers a framework of eight vital achievements that took him to a state of personal and vocational flourishing.

Behind this book's covers, he dives into these mile markers, unveils a blueprint and shares personal stories to help guide and equip other freelancers in their difficult but rewarding journey.

Learn more at www.pathofthefreelancer.com

www.ingramcontent.com/pod-product-compliance
Lightning Source LLC
Chambersburg PA
CBHW021809170526
45157CB00007B/2517